Open Spaces: M
Mountain Chief,

Blackfeet Elder from Northwest Montana

By Jay North aka J Mountain Chief

1st edition 2002

Revised 2014

ISBN-13: 9781463619497
ISBN-10: 1463619499

Come Into Sacred Ceremony with Leonard and Jay

Flowing is Spirit Talk with Leonard, enjoy.

Open Spaces Book Reviews

Jay,
I am in tears of joy. Wow! Not only do you write so
beautifully, but about something I can relate to. The Pipe
Ceremony! How fitting. The words you've written are so
pure and true... I had an eagle experience last summer along
the Trinity River. I smoked the sacred pipe and raised my
arms to the sky in triangle pose, glancing beyond my
fingertips to the heavens, and there was the bald eagle
soaring in circles high above. I prayed. A minute later the
mergansers quacked there way upriver. Great Spirit was ever
so present. I cried tears of deep emotions, and every time I
had a breakthrough Spirit showed itself in Nature. I was
overwhelmed with joy. I became reawakened and in tune
with God, Great Spirit, Creator. This is what my songs are
about...the ones I sing and the ones that come through me.
Music flows through me. I hear it, especially when I'm in
tune. (Lyrics don't come as easily to me, so I often just have
tunes, or only part of a song's lyrics.) It is the feeling that is
the soul of the song. The music is a gift. Being guided on the
path, living the prayer is the ultimate gift. I have strong faith,
yet I seek clarity of the path ahead. In these times of turmoil I
seek companionship, community, oneness with nature and
oneness with Creator. I choose the path of healing, love and
service. I have no name for the path, for there are many. The
red path is one I have chosen.

I greatly respect you. I give thanks and praise for being
touched by you.
With deep Love and Respect, Mitzi

±

I never met Leonard J. Mountain Chief, yet his spirit
is closely entwined with mine and I call him brother and I

call him friend. This book is more than just the story of the close friendship of two men; it carries forth the spirit of Leonard J. Mountain Chief in such a way that the reader finds themselves feeling a kinship, a brotherhood with him as our mutual God, our father binds us together.

This book carries forth the spirit of the Native Americans. As Leonard and Jay have their adventures, we don't just read about them, we experience them. Although he tells this book in the first person and it is indeed a book about the experiences that Jay had with this his foster father, Jay North has done a tremendous job in allowing us to experience for ourselves the man who was and who is, for his spirit lives on, Leonard J. Mountain Chief.

I highly recommend this book, not just for those of us who are Native Americans, but for all people everywhere. I personally have been greatly blessed by it.

Bunny Gail McLeod, VT.

±

CHA WAKAN Jay,   I'm enjoying reading your book Open Spaces very much! As I am reading about your life's journey; " its apparently becomes Indian time to me!"

 I found myself falling into your stories with my whole body. I can scene myself right there, watching and anticipating in silence," what will come next"?

Great Job!! Aho, Mitakuye Oyasin Catrina Oyasin Santa Barbara, CA

±

Jay North captures the heart of the Native Montana, the wisdom of the people who nurture and are preserved by the land of their ancestors. Montana speaks to these people in loving instruction spoken in the words of nature. Interpreted through the knowingness of an honored chief, father and profound friend. In Open Spaces: My Life with Leonard Mountain Chief, Jay imparts his experience living on the Blackfeet reservation. Jay had the privilege of walking with the kindness of Leonard and becoming his adopted son; and as fathers do, Leonard initiated Jay into the mindfulness of these Montana Native people. With great generosity, Jay shares with his readers his private communion with his Blackfeet mentor. The delivery of the messages is shared with the tone of Jay's own given name by Leonard Mountain chief, "With Heart Wide Open". As with all oral tradition, the reader learns and softens to the spoken word of the natural spirit through this loving and appreciative heart of Heart Butte, the heart of the author, Jay North.

Susan Del Nagro

±

Reading Open Spaces was a true joy. Although Jay was telling "his" story, it also became mine as I became a part of the adventures, a part of the journey that he shares with the reader. I felt as if Leonard was my father, teaching me the wisdom of the people. I shared in Jay's joy with laughter and in his sadness with tears. This is one of the best writings I have been blessed to read. Jay writes with humor, candidness and respect. I cannot recommend it highly enough to anyone interested in the native culture or anyone who is open enough to learn the message of this book. Sandra Alevras, Chicago Il.

±

Jay and I ventured out to Leonard's on many occasions to fly fish the Lower Two Medicine River together and visit Jay's beloved friend, father and guide. I grew to know Leonard and acquired an understanding of Jay's deep respect and reference for this holy man I am truly grateful for the experience and the connection, Thank you Jay, well done on telling these story's Dave Yates MD. Charlotte NC

±

Book review by Jim Carey

In January of 1999, I had just retired, sold almost all I owned, and started my personal spiritual journey. I'd been a scientist and a rationalist all of my life but had found that science couldn't answer the really interesting questions. So I left science and engineering to pursue my search for Truth.

In that pursuit, I've read hundreds of books, listened to dozens of lectures, and surprised myself as I evolved from religionist to theologian to philosopher.

Which brings me to Jay North's book?

When I was handed this book as a 200-page typed, double-spaced manuscript, I took it home expecting to breeze through it in a couple of hours. Instead, it took me two weeks to digest. I could only read a few pages at a time before I had to stop and think about the message Jay was sharing. Very few books move me that way.

In my spiritual research, I was attracted to American Indian spiritual lore, but until I read this book, I'd found little documentation of the broad overview that this book gives and none so clearly and simply written.

What I found in this book was an excellent summary of my last seven years of philosophical studies. I've reached an outlook on the Nature of the Universe that is virtually identical with that of Leonard J. Mountain Chief, Blackfeet Elder.

I found, much to my surprise, that after all that research and study, I've finally reached the level of Spiritual Consciousness that the Blackfeet Indians achieved centuries ago.

Before reading this book, I also believed that in one's search for Truth, one must trod the path through Plato, Aristotle, Aristophanes, Zarathustra, Krishna, Buddha, Abraham, Moses, David, Jesus, Francis of Assisi, Aquinas, Moore, Szekely, Redfield, Dyer, Hawkins, et. Al., in order to reach the conclusions I've reached.

Instead, Jay gives us the summary in short, clear words, as given by his mentor, Chief Leonard. This is the summary and concise statements that I didn't think existed.

Following are some excerpts from *Open Spaces: My Life with Leonard J. Mountain Chief, Blackfeet Elder from Northwest Montana.*

"Just as a dieter will regain weight after they come off of the diet and resume their old eating habits, the seeker of real change must be willing to make a real lifestyle change. It is easy to be enthusiastic for a short period of time to achieve a goal, but the true test of commitment will be a change of the heart… a life of service."

"Everything is perfect all of the time, even when you don't think it is."

"… Our true purpose for being here … is Love and the true unfoldment of the Spirit … there is no higher purpose than to love another ... We cannot simply examine this thing; we must experience it in order to fulfill our destiny."

"Spirit always looks after you."

"Now is a time of paramount importance for all people to hear the message of loving each other and our world, the message of being at peace with one another and our world, and the message of finding joy in each other and in our world."

Thank you, Jay North, for sharing your experiences with Chief Leonard with us. How blessed you were to have them! Every Spiritual Seeker should read this book and become enlightened by it. I find in it... Truth. The world needs to read this book.

Jim Carey

All pictures and photographs available in color at www.OneGlobePress.com

***Open Spaces: My Life with Leonard J. Mountain
Chief, Blackfeet Elder from Northwestern Montana***
by Jay North aka J Mountain Chief

Eight-year-old Jay North read a book about Montana
that changed his life. Ever precocious and constantly
curious, young Jay decided that this rugged outback
was a path he would one day travel. True to his
dream, Jay eventually traveled to the Treasure State
and met a true diamond in the rough, Blackfeet tribal
elder Leonard J. Mountain Chief.

After Jay's retirement from *Paradise Farms*--his organic farm in Carpinteria California, he and his beloved late wife Pamela (Pammy) made the huge move to the Big Sky country of his boyhood dreams.

From their first 1990 encounter in Jay's quaint Native American Art shop until Leonard's passing in 1999, Jay recounts his decade of deliverance in his newest work, entitled **Open Spaces: My Life with Leonard J. Mountain Chief, Blackfeet Elder from Northwestern Montana**. This intimate collection of 28 stories about Leonard's unique visions and teachings is framed by the adventures of these two exceptional individuals.

Blackfeet elder Leonard J. Mountain Chief served in the US army and fought two wars for this country's freedom, the Second World War and the Korean War, retiring with medals of Honor. Returning to the United States and his beloved mountain, Heart Butte, he served on the tribal counsel for over 25 years and was instrumental figurehead among his tribe.

Leonard was also a remarkable artisan, a world-class fiddler, a tribal storyteller, and actor. As the tribe's storyteller, teacher and heritage passer, he preserved the traditional Indian way for generations to come. He was a strong, courageous man, huge in stature and spirit. Filled with remarkable experiences of sacred ceremonies, wilderness journeys and inspired conversations, the Big Sky country serves as both the storyboard and the setting of Leonard's beloved home in Heart Butte, Montana.

Native American spirituality teachers are

increasingly sought after, and literature by these historical gatekeepers continues to be highly popular, demonstrating a lively and enduring following. The Northwest Montana Blackfeet Indian Reservation is home to the magnificent people of the Blackfeet and Blackfoot nations. Proud of their notorious stature as fierce warriors, they were among the last Native people to fight for freedom, finally subdued in 1894. Today they call Glacier National Park home, the motherland of these determined people.

Jay North is a self-taught organic farmer and one of the country's leading experts and originators in the organic industry. Over the last thirty years, Jay has developed and promoted a nationally recognized farm, assisted hundreds of clients in the marketing of their products, and grown and promoted a wide array of innovative, organically grown farm products. His work has been featured in newspapers, magazines, and on national radio and television, including the *Today Show*, the *Tonight Show* and many others. He is an accomplished writer, author, and expert on organic farming practices, publishing several popular titles, including *Getting Started in Organic Gardening For Fun and Profit*, *Guide to Cooking with Edible Flowers*, *The Gift of Touch* and *Miracles In The Kitchen* Jay is also the proprietor of GoingOrganic.com, a one-stop-shop for consultations, design assistance, learning, literature and other tools to explore the possibilities of organic farming, for both beginners as well as large-scale operations.www.GoingOrganic.com Jay's books are available at http://www.OneGlobePress.com

Jay is also a practitioner in the healing arts and his book **The Gift of Touch** teaches his modalities for healing people.

Leonard always said "your path is your own and your challenge is to find it". Jay North once read a book (Black Elk Speaks) that changed his life. Now he wants the world to read **Open Spaces: My Life with Leonard J. Mountain Chief, Blackfeet Elder from Northwestern Montana**, and have the same transcendent experience. As Leonard would say, 'Ah Uh Op Vista Doggie, Vista Doggie Ah He; God Bless you God Bless us All.

Jay's books are available at of his websites, www.OneGlobePress.com and at www.Amazon.com

Table of Contents

Important note to readers:

Grandfather Sun; hear my prayers, let these words be heard and understood.

Often when Leonard spoke and wanted to make a point very clear and particularly important, he would often say, "There is nothing else" or "there is nothing else as important". Often you will see the phrase "there is no other way". I left these statements intact to do my best to convey Leonard's attempt to stress things in his teachings. I apologize ahead of time if you find these repeated statements bothersome in any way.

One other point I would like you to consider in reading this book: I have done my very best to accurately convey these messages without too much explanation. Leonard liked people to do their own thinking without him having to say too much. I did the same here as well. As Leonard often repeated, "Do not speak, it only wastes energy." Yes, he spoke, just not all that often. He would tell his stories and be brief about it. He wanted listeners to walk away asking their own questions and listening for the answers in their own heart. I hope you find these stories useful in your life and that you are able to apply the lessons for yourself, as I have tried to do in mine. Then I will know that I have done my job.

When you find yourself wanting to know exactly what the scenes looked like, and if you happen to think the picture isn't painted quite clearly enough for you to get, close your eyes, do not speak, but imagine.

Jay and His Love for Organic Gardening

Two Medicine Range:

The People have used this location for vision quest for over 14,000 years. They saw the whites coming from this vantage point long before they arrived.

Foreword

The Northwest Montana, Blackfeet Indian Reservation is a magnificent place where The People of the Blackfeet Nation have been doing vision quests for over 14,000 years.

The Blackfeet prided themselves on being fierce, bloodthirsty warriors and fighters. They were among the very last Native people to fight for their freedom until they were subdued by the U.S. Army in 1894, in the burnt mountains of what is now called Glacier National Park.

To this day, they are a strong, proud tribe, who believe that they will win back their freedom and independence, even as government restraints, controls, and practices continue to make life rough for all indigenous people in the U.S.

But that is not what this book is about. Native people believe in fighting their own battles and I'm not going to take one up here. This book is about my adopted father, Blackfeet elder Leonard J. Mountain Chief, and the teaching, guidance, and warm love he shared with me—and has for all of humanity.

Leonard was named after his great-grandfather of the Piegan, the original tribe name of The People of northwest Montana or, more accurately, from the entire region now known as Montana, before they were "settled."

The Blackfeet/Blackfoot, as they became known, once occupied and fought for a very large section of North America that included all of Montana, parts of southern Canada, northern Wyoming, eastern Idaho and the western Dakotas.

Leonard was a strong, courageous man, huge in stature and in spirit. He was a world-class fiddler, a tribal storyteller, and an actor. He was husband to his beautiful wife, Dee, father of two children with Dee, and adopted father to Charlie, my Native brother, and me.

Leonard served in the U.S. army and fought two wars for this country, the Second World War and the Korean War. He left the army with medals and honor. His war days done, he returned to his beloved mountain, Heart Butte, where he bought land back on the Reservation from some white people who had bought a piece and legally and owned it free and clear. Leonard wanted to own the place he would call home for the rest of his life. We used to tease about the remoteness of the place, calling it 45 minutes from a quart of milk, because that's how long it usually took to drive into town on a good day to buy one. In the winter, forget it.

Leonard served on the tribal counsel for over 25 years and was instrumental in leading The People towards industriousness and away from drugs and alcohol. He participated in all tribal events, except when he was away making a film or fiddling at the Grand Ole Opry.

The violin was his passion, and he played like no one you have ever heard. He was also the tribe's storyteller, teacher, and heritage passer, which meant he was responsible for keeping and passing on the traditional Indian way. And that is how we were to meet and become very close friends.

Leonard was an extremely jovial man, except in times when reverence was called for. He loved to laugh, and he had a trickster coyote's sense of humor. He was a wonderful and patient teacher. He never scolded me—not even once. He would, on occasion, give me instructions to follow for this or that purpose, but never once was he forceful or impatient for me to get a point or make a decision. My direction was always my own and I was never made to feel small or wrong for my choices.

Respect and freedom of choice were values dear to Leonard, and it was important to him to teach these values to others. How much better all our lives could and would be if we embraced these two ideals! Leonard taught these as he did everything he believed in—with patience and without malice.

Leonard well understood the importance of choices and never forced his ideas on me, or anyone that I ever witnessed. He had his opinions, don't get me wrong, but as he used to say, "We all have opinions, and they are all worth a nickel." He always said, "Your path is your own and your challenge is to find it."

This book is dedicated to Leonard, his family, The People of the Nations, and to all those who seek unfoldment of the soul. Special thanks to my beloved late wife, Pamela, whose encouragement and allowance gave me the time and space to be with Leonard J. Mountain Chief and learn the Native way.

Also special thanks to Dona Haber, Bunny (Gail) McLeod, Christy Wilson, Amanda Mashburn and Ramona Peet for their editing and contributions. Most of all thank you Leonard for your love patience, and guidance. And particular thanks to Malcolm Watson, world-renowned violinist, for encouraging me to write these stories. I hope that people everywhere enjoy them and will be able to apply these lessons in your own life, as I have for many years. Come into Sacred Ceremony with Jay and Leonard...

Thank you Pamela, my deceased former wife, who patiently encouraged my relationship with my mentor, Leonard J. Mountain Chief

Note: No doubt readers of this material will find incorrect grammar and often slang words. I have left the language this way for two reasons. First, Leonard and other natives I came to know speak in broken English, and secondly, I wanted to keep the stories REAL for my readers.

Leonard always gave thanks to Great Spirit and often referred to him as Grandfather or Grandfather Sun. Many times, although not repeated in this manuscript; he would give praises to the ancestors and asked for their guidance and power.

Please know that I desire, require, and request your help in making these stories known to your friends and family. Please tell as many people as you would like to about the book, and ask them to go directly to my website to purchase a copy. People will find this and other books I have written on the books page on my website www.OneGlobePress.com

Return to Open Spaces: The Final Chapter—it is done, finally 2014!

The Following is Spirit Talk with Leonard J. Mountain Chief

*Grand Father Sun, hear my words and
deliver them to the people…*

Church in the Native Way; Great Spirit Take Pity On US

Great Spirit, (Napi) Almighty Healer and Creator of all
things, with humbled hearts we gather together to offer
up many thanks. We thank you for the flowing waters
from the mountaintop as it slowly makes its way to the
valley below. We thank you for the mighty Eagle as it
soars overhead. We thank you for Brother Bear as he
fishes for his food in the early morning hour. We thank
you for the song of the mourning dove as she perches
upon the limb. We thank you for the ants as they show
us the importance of working together to get the task
done. For the grace of the ocean waves as they rush to
the shoreline, we thank you. For the unique paths and
purpose you have given us, we give thanks. We thank

you for the many gifts and blessings you have bestowed upon your people.

We ask for mercy and forgiveness for those that are addicted to materialism, power, wealth and those things that are harmful to our physical being. We ask for an end to the wanton desire for nuclear power, for it generates more harm to your creation than to our want for its energy. We ask for an end to the division that separates the four colors. We ask instead for a time of unity so we may begin to repair the damage we have done to your creation. We ask for an end to the abuse and killing of the defenseless animals that surround us. We ask for veils of secrecy to finally open so that your light may penetrate the darkness of deceit. We ask for all, like our Brother Leonard Peltier, who have been incarcerated unjustly, to be granted freedom to return to their land and families. We ask for an end to domestic violence and abuse being perpetrated against our women and children. We ask for protection and freedom for those of our children that have been abducted. We ask for great healing for those that are suffering through diverse diseases and disorders. We ask for your guidance and strength as we stand against those that continue to bring destruction upon your creation. We ask for courage to be given to those that have heard your call, during this time of change, but are apprehensive about performing the acts you have given.

We thank you for our Elders that continue to bring us the lessons of the present as well as the wisdom of the past. We thank you for our children that will one day understand all they have been given and pass them onto the next generation. We thank you for our daily food and ask for its blessing. We thank you for the air we breathe and the waters that hydrate our bodies. We thank you for the awakening of spirits that are now forming as Rainbow Tribe Warriors throughout Mother Earth to bring back balance. Great Spirit teach us how to walk in a good way and love more! Aho.

Just South of Leonard's Place, Starting the Plains on the Res

Chapter 1
There Is Nothing Else

While living in Northwest Montana for a good long time I came to know, love, and be adopted by Leonard J. Mountain Chief, a well known and highly respected elder of the Blackfeet tribe.

Our First Meeting: I was co-owner, along with my late wife Pamela, of Bull Trading Co., an art gallery in Kalispell, Montana just west of the Rockies and south of Canada. It was a small, funky shop in a small, funky town. We specialized in Native American art and collectibles. Leonard got word about our store through a mutual friend, and he came to visit late one summer afternoon in 1990.

Jay's and Pammy's Gallery in Kalispell, MT

Through a large picture window at the front of the gallery, I saw two Native folks drive up in front of the store. Something told me Leonard was an important figure to his tribe, so I immediately began to put together a bundle to offer him as a gift when he walked through the door. This was a custom of The People that I already knew, and I was soon to learn that Leonard was a man of long history and deep tradition.

Leonard was an extremely large, handsome man and carried himself tall and proud. He had reddish-brown skin and flecks of silver in his black hair. When we shook hands and I gave him the bundle filled with sage, tobacco, sweet grass, turquoise, and feathers. He said, "We are to be good friends of long standing, you and me."

I agreed, and we visited for many hours that day. How glad I am, and will always be, that his prediction became a reality.

Leonard was the storyteller and heritage-passer for the Piegan, the Native name of the tribe. He loved to tell Indian stories and fiddle on his violin, and I was a welcoming audience for him and his tales of knee-high grass and the buffalo meat that fed his ancestors for centuries. I was never bored, never tired, and showed only the deepest respect for him and his heritage.

At the end of his visit that first night, Leonard bid me farewell by inviting me out to his place, east of the divide, in Heart Butte, also known as Old Agency. "So, you're a fly fisherman," he said.

"Yes, I am," I replied.

"Good," he said, "my land has the best. Come stay with me awhile." This I did several times each year for many years to follow.

The drive along the edge of Glacier National Park from west to east over to Heart Butte is incredibly beautiful. The tall pines, the cottonwoods, the aspens, the wild elk, deer, moose and geese flying overhead, give one the feeling of being in a storybook. It's almost surreal, but, at the same time, very real. And, oh, so peaceful. Rarely a chore to be done except in the winter as you will learn later.

Big Horned Sheep — A Common Sight in Glacier National Park

I was headed for Two Medicine River to fish, and I arrived at Leonard's home late one afternoon. As I turned right off the cut-a-cross road,

View from Leonard's Land, Back to the "Cut-across" Road from East Glacier to Heart Butte

I could see Leonard sitting on the porch of his small wooden house in an old wicker chair. I waved and he waved me on, knowing exactly where I was headed. I knew he wouldn't be far behind. Leonard could never turn down a cup of my coffee or an ear for his storytelling.

His stories always had meaning, even when it wasn't clear to me what the meaning was until he was finished. Many times, even today, I find myself pondering the meaning of his tales, his examples, and his life. Often things are much deeper than they seem to be on the surface.

Jay Fly-fishing down at His Spot on Two Medicine River, 1000 yards below Leonard's House

One of the very first things Leonard taught me was to go out and find a spot. A spot in nature is important, he said, for a sense of self and a sense of purpose. It's a place to call your own, even if you have no deed to the property. A spot can be anywhere you go to learn about the world, yourself, the rest of existence, and the deeper meaning of life. Leonard was the only person I ever shared my spot with.

When I arrived at my spot in the bottom of the canyon on the Two Medicine River about six p.m., I put up my tent and cook stove and started some coffee. I was eager to get to the evening bite of the rising trout, which were plentiful on Leonard's stretch of the river, because no one ever fishes there except me. Best of all, these fish aren't fly shy, which is to say they'll eat just about anything you toss at 'em.

Leonard showed up not long afterwards, "Got any coffee brewing?" he asked.

"Yes, Leonard, of course. Want a cup?" Leonard didn't drink beverages with alcohol—hadn't for many years. "Have a seat, Leonard. Let me pour you a cup."

Leonard liked his coffee strong and black. With his coffee in hand, he took center stage and began telling stories of long ago. I fixed dinner, and Leonard told stories; I made another pot of coffee, and Leonard told stories. Please understand two things. One, these are stories are of immense importance to the tribe, and two, out of pure respect, one listens intently. But I had come to fish, as well.

"Well you know, Leonard," I said, "We should get some rest because in the morning I'm going to want to fish some." I looked at my watch, and hell, it was already morning. I shrugged. So much for sleep! "The sun will be up in about half an hour," I said. You want some breakfast?"

"Sure," Leonard replied, "and how about some more of that great coffee?"

We ate, I got my fly-fishing gear together and we were off. Leonard doesn't fish, never has. We walked the river for a few hours in a wondrously beautiful canyon, with wildflowers on the cliffs and plenty of hungry trout in the clear water.

I fished, Leonard told stories. We walked, talked, fished, ate, and for three days I listened with pure enchantment to Native wisdom.

We had been on the river for three days and nights when I said to Leonard, "I should think about heading back west to Kalispell in the morning. Pammy will be wondering where I have been off to and will want know I'm okay. And Dee, Leonard? Won't she be worried about you?" I asked.

"No, hell," he said. "She knows I go off for several days on my own, by-golly, same as you do, Jay. Your wife knows where you are and that you're doing what you love."

We had our last meal of the trip together that night. Some of the stories Leonard told brought tears to my eyes. Some made me laugh. Some made me think—and all were very much appreciated, because I had Leonard all to myself, teaching me about the Indian ways of long ago.

I caught plenty of trout—let most of 'em go, and Leonard and I enjoyed eating a few together.

When Leonard and I finished our meal, it was about one a.m. We walked out to the water's edge, looking northwest up the Two Medicine River Canyon. A full moon was rising over the Lewis and Clark Mountain Range, just below Glacier National Park, and it came shining down through the pine trees onto the water. There was the smell of cottonwood, pine and sage in crystal-clear air. The moon was bright as the sun. We stood there silent, watching, listening to the night sounds — the crackling fire from the camp, running water and howling coyotes. We stood quietly together for about forty-five minutes, neither of us speaking a word. Then Leonard looked over his right shoulder to me and ever so quietly said, "There is nothing else, Jay. There is nothing else."

I replied, "Leonard, no. There is nothing else."

In 1997, I finished my vision quest. Leonard became my adopted Father, and my love for him and my people will never die.

Here are just is a sampling of our stories, Enjoy.

Chapter 2
Walking the Red Path

When one embarks on the Red Path, one must become dedicated to it, and this will lead to the highest goal, the unfoldment of the soul. The precepts of walking the Red Path are not unlike spiritual principles followed by people of other cultures and traditions throughout the world. It requires dedication, persistence, and most of all, patience.

One of the first principles is to be conscious of your days and where you are. Leonard taught me that your life isn't something that is *going to happen* or something that *might happen* — your life is *everything that happens.* It is now. "It takes place even while you're waiting for something great to occur," said Leonard. "Life is in each moment, whether you are looking at it or not."

Walking the Red Path requires one to quiet the mind and listen; it is taught that even the wind will carry a message. One on the path who listens will hear messages, this is certain. And the messages will bring of unfoldment and new realization.

Jay and Pammy's Land, Back Forty in Kalispell, MT

Leonard taught that revitalizing oneself is what enables us to be what we need to be. If we have not fed ourselves, we will not have the energy to feed others. If we have not gotten to know ourselves, we will never be able to know others. We cannot teach others if we have not stopped to learn for ourselves. If we do not refresh ourselves mentally, physically and spiritually, we will be of no use to the ones we most dearly love. To nurture another, we have to first nurture ourselves.

"Leonard," I asked, "how often do I need to be alone, and for how long? How do I find time to be alone with all the other commitments I have in my busy, modern life?"

Leonard replied, "Drop what you consider reality in modern life. Just stop everything and find a way to nurture yourself. How long does it take for this nurturing to happen and for you to feel as though you actually got something out of it? A day or two? A week or two? Years? It's up to you."

Leonard taught that it is of vital importance for the student of the Red Path to pay particular attention to the Earth and her elements and to recognize our connection to her and to the sun, the stars, the moon, and most of all, the Great Spirit — Grandfather Sun.

Moose on the Middle Fork of the Flathead River

No doubt some will say that listening to messages from the four directions, East, North, West, and South, is nothing more than superstition, but we recognize that the four elements, fire, earth, wind and water carry significant messages, as do the four directions. If we pay particular attention, answers to long-awaited questions will come to us and lead us closer to hearing the words of The Great Spirit himself and to the unfoldment of our soul.

Many walking the Red Path hear the words of deceased elders and the elders are often called upon for guidance, as are the stories of old that help to unravel and reveal basic truths that guide our paths today. Many hear messages in dance and song. It is through rituals that we come to know ourselves and many great truths, but, as Leonard taught, you can hear nothing if you never stop to listen.

Walking the Red Path requires dedication, faith and reverence; and no one should begin the walk lightheartedly, said Leonard.

Many may seek a teacher, but one's teacher tends to come by what is called an intentional accident, for when the mind of the student is ready, a teacher will appear, as the lessons of Little Badger or Morning Star illustrate.

Our totems come when the student's mind is ready to accept their teaching, and if the lesson is absorbed, one may find his or her life elevated to a point of new understanding and discover the ability to be closer to the Great One and even to heal oneself and possibly others too.

In Leonard's stories and the Blackfeet people's teachings, I learned that in order to unfold in our true destiny with happiness and joy, we must find out exactly who we are and come to know our purpose for being here. It is taught that it is our right to know these things. "We came here to Know."

One day Leonard said to me, "You know, my boy, it was no accident we met. We have known one another for a very long time and we have come together to walk the Red Path once more, to realize our great strength as one, and to help guide the way for many others.

"Through our mutual love and respect we will come to know one another well. We will travel; we will sing, dance and pray. We will share many sorrows and joys and will come to better know the Great Spirit and feel his presence ever closer day by day.

"You will meet many great leaders of The People," Leonard said, "and they will share their stories with you. You will come to know the elders who have left this place and you will be able to communicate with the beings we hold in high regard. Do this in joy, but also in reverence, for it is through your deep love, respect and reverence for The People that your unfoldment will come.

"Walking the Red Path requires courage, determination and strength," he said, "and once you begin to walk the path, you will find you will be on it until its end. That is the great mystery. It will provide the answers you are calling for. It is up to you to walk, quiet yourself, listen, and follow.

"Many lessons," he continued, "are told in riddles and poems. Some of your questions may be answered by a bush or a bug. We have been storytellers for a very long time, and we rely on the stories of old to reveal the new. We tell stories to encourage you to use your own mind. We want you to make your own decisions for your life and the unfoldment of your own path. If all mysteries were told to you or put on your plate all at once, you would not see them, nor believe what you were looking at.

"Your path into the great unknown and the unfoldment of truth is a gradual process, and with patience and dedication, everything you want to know will come.

People have too many projections. "I have no rules and regulations set in place for you to follow. I ask only that you agree to allow the truths to come and that you recognize them as they come. Follow the way with the gifts presented to you. Walk through life with these gifts, but never in a pious way.

"You will come into ceremony with us. We will smoke the pipe and we will go deep into trance with our dance, and if you come to find the Red Path a difficult and arduous adventure, try not to give in to weakness and fall away. You will find that what you came to find out from me and The People is just right around the corner, and if you fall off the path you will miss this entirely.

"Walking the Red Path is not for the weak man. It takes quiet determination and persistent asking of questions that have been in all men's minds for many thousands of years.

"You may ask, 'how do we know of these things and what certainty can you have in the truths about to unfold to you? After all, the Indians were defeated by the White man.' Yes, it is true. We saw this coming long before it occurred, and it has been part of our unfoldment, not unlike that of the Tibetans with the Chinese. It was part of our path to experience these things. The path and the mysteries unfold themselves. When we look and listen, we shall know.

"And what purpose does this serve?" he asked. "Be patient, watch, listen, and you will know. It is about the unfoldment of the soul and walking your path."

While I am certain Leonard's unfoldment did occur, I yet am on the path, and Leonard's guidance lives with me even today, and I am reminded to listen for Grandfather's voice.

Chapter 3
If You Listen, My Friend

Leonard asked that I quiet my mind and listen. He said, "If you listen, my friend, even the wind will tell you a story. My people have been taught the ways of man by nature for thousands of years. Everything in nature has a story and a lesson, and your job is to listen. What you do with it is your choice.

"Listen to the wind; it will unfold your path for you. Pray, fast and sweat, find your totem in the wolf, coyote, bear, and squirrel.

"Turn your attention to the north. Watch the colors and movement of the northern lights. They reveal the way to travel and when to stay put."

The advice from Leonard J. Mountain Chief and the way of the Nation was always clear. Be quiet, listen and watch. Quiet your mind. Do not speak—it only wastes energy.

Leonard advised me to go to the top of the mountain and sit quietly for a week, fasting, chanting, praying and listening. He said, "Your name, my boy, is 'One with Heart Foolishly Wide Open'."

"Leonard, explain to me what you mean by 'One with Heart Foolishly Wide Open,'" I asked.

"My boy," he answered, "to love everyone is good, but you do not discern well. Open love is good, but it can break your heart when you love foolishly.

The 100-Year Storm blew in at 70 degrees Below Zero, January 1990. Welcome to Montana. Leonard predicted this storm coming three weeks before it arrived.

"Now go, sit, and find your path with that heart of yours. Watch the animals. Observe their movements and actions. Imitate them. Hear the voice of the animal that speaks to you most clearly. Follow whatever he tells you to do, even if you think it is wrong. If you heard him with your heart and not your ears, he is not wrong and will never mislead you.

"After you have fasted and spoken with your totem animals, go into the sweat lodge. Be there for several days. When you have sweated out all of your wrongdoings and doubt, come out and breathe in the four directions. Ask each to confirm your new path. Eat a hearty meal. Light a fire, dance, sing, and scream, for now you know your way. Give thanks and praise to the Creator for having given you the animals to teach you what man could not."

Leonard never let up on the importance of knowing one's path, one's life's work. Where one should *be* is of paramount importance in Indian life. *Being* in Native terms is where one stays for any given length of time.

Even though we all live everywhere, we stay here or there for periods of time, in a space, held in place by the belief that this is where we are supposed to be at that time. That's why accepting reservation life was hard for the Blackfeet. They were not certain that the Res was where they were supposed to be. And, of course, there was always the question, "Will there be enough buffalo meat here to feed our people?"

In contemporary days and in our hurried lives we can now and then forget where we are supposed to be. We can forget who we are and we somehow manage to get off our path, even after we think we have it all figured out. We can forget our purposes and sacrifice them for lesser goals, money, and things.

Leonard was here to remind me, "No doubt in this society you have to earn, you have a family and responsibilities, you have a job or business, and you have obligations to your community and the elders of your tribe. But remember, my boy, your only real obligation is to the Creator and to live the purpose that He gave to you when He sent you here."

Leonard taught me to never to attempt to be liked or admired. No matter what anyone tells you or thinks of what you do, your path or purpose is your own, and you have to live by your own standards- not anyone else's.

Leonard was a great teacher of integrity and honesty. He was a powerful man who knew his own strength and power. He never abused it; he simply knew who he was and he never disparaged himself to win friends or votes.

Honesty and integrity were his badge of honor. Though his tribe and those with the pleasure of knowing him gave him the honor of respect, his true honor was in how he lived and the example he set. His legacy of teaching and helping others continues with those he taught, helped and, touched.

"My friend, go find your spot, watch, and listen," he told me. "It's in the wind; you will hear it. Listen to the quiet, and in the quiet you will find many answers, answers about yourself and others around you. Answers to questions you never thought to ask. The quiet speaks—and what it says is worth volumes of words. Do not speak it; it would only waste energy," he said.

Note: Every Totem animal has special meaning only to its seer.

A Small Herd of Doe Deer Up on the Knoll at Leonard's Place

Chapter 4
Forgiveness

Leonard and I often took long, slow walks in the hills around Heart Butte. As we walked, he loved to tell Indian stories of long ago. Often he would start them with, "When the grass was knee high..."

Leonard saw, as many of us do, too much needless suffering. One day while we were walking, he spoke of forgiveness.

"When we look around the world today, we find much needless suffering," he said. "The causes are indeed vast. People everywhere are hurt, lonely, and depressed. Some are just starving for a simple hug."

He went on to say that people's lives could be changed and improved through the act of forgiveness. "While this may be a foreign concept for some," he said, "it will be easy for others to grasp and apply to their lives, to help promote a new outlook and experience.

"I hope you will see the value of forgiveness in your life," he said. "I believe that people can understand that they can actually be free, simply through the act of forgiveness. Recall Christ's words, 'Forgive them, Father, for they know not what they do.' Christ's love for all humanity was so strong that even in his own deep suffering all he could consider was forgiveness."

"Native people have been confronting this subject and dealing with issues connected to forgiveness for many years," said Leonard. "We can choose to excuse or forgive our enemies, so called evil ones, spouses for wrongdoings or mistakes made against us, however perceived. We can forgive our neighbors and live in peace.

"There is no doubt that there is a world of hurt all around us," he went on. "As each and every person, group and clan has some perceived vision of being wronged, we can feel victimized occasionally by those who wish to oppress us in one way or another. Throughout history, for many thousands of years, people have felt taken advantage of, hurt, used, and abused. It goes beyond feelings. It touches on our core of beliefs, emotions, and the very basic trusts we have in people around us. Somehow, many feel that they have been betrayed.

"But what if, just perhaps, our own experience can be made more pleasurable? What if it can become easier to get along, live well, and prosper beyond our current circumstance if we can learn to forgive? What if this is possible?"

Referring to the tribe's hatred of Whites, Leonard said, "If we can learn to forgive the White man, we'll all be better off. It is time for us to forgive and move on."

"But Leonard," I asked, "How can you tell me to forgive someone who has done me a horrible wrong? What if this person murdered my child or raped me or cheated my family out of our money?"

"Forgive them," he said.

This heartfelt conversation with Leonard brought to mind an incident at a concert in Los Angeles that my then beautiful African-American girlfriend and I were attending. The concert was intended primarily for an African-American audience, and a young man approached my companion and asked her, "What are you doing with this honky?" We were holding hands.

I stepped in to answer for her, "Look man, I'm not a honky any more than you are a Negro. If you cut me, you will see I am exactly like you. And if you are cut, you will see you are exactly like me. We will both bleed. We are the same. We both appreciate a beautiful woman, it's time we forgive one another's race and move on, for we are, in fact, brothers."

He stood silent for a moment and laughed and agreed. We hugged and that was the last I saw of him, and no other negative events happened that night.

Leonard said, "Humans can find all sorts of supposedly justifiable reasons to hate one another. Out of fear-based conclusions that create our barriers, we have held on to the separation instead of actually loving one another and realizing our oneness in The Great Spirit.

"The lack of forgiving rarely harms the person one refuses to forgive. The real harm is done to the one who refuses to forgive. Hatred, bitterness, and grudges eat away at the soul of one holding them inside, said Leonard.

"What many fail to realize about forgiveness is that if the person deserves to be forgiven, it isn't forgiveness! Forgiveness is a unique act reserved for those who have harmed us, either intentionally or unintentionally, and who do not deserve to be excused for their actions.

"When we are wronged," he said, "we have a choice: to forgive or not to forgive. Forgiving, truly forgiving, is difficult. We must surrender our right to hold a wrong against an offender. It defies our human need to defend ourselves and avenge ourselves."

He went on, "The alternative is un-forgiveness. Let's take a look at that decision. When we fail to forgive our offenders, we hold something harmful within ourselves. This ugly thing isn't in them—it is in us. We carry it. We become frustrated because we see the person who has done us wrong, and they seem fine. They are happy and going about their business while we, the offended, are often ill and miserable.

"Frustration leads, as any psychologist will tell you, to anger. Anger is either expressed, causing further harm to others, who in turn are confronted with the decision to forgive or not to forgive, or it is turned inward. Do you know what psychologists call 'anger turned inward'? Depression!" he said.

"I know of no human, male or female, black, white, red, or brown, young or old, rich or poor, who has never been wronged. Every one of us will face the decision to forgive at some point in our lives—and most of us will face it many times over. Will we forgive, releasing our offender—but more—releasing ourselves from the bondage of hatred? Or, will we become frustrated, angry, and depressed or lash out, leaving a fresh trail of hurt across humankind?

"Forgiving is hard. It requires us to let go of our right to avenge those who have hurt us. The alternative is easier, but vastly more destructive," said Leonard.

"But not all is hopeless," Leonard continued. "If we decide and if we choose, we can evolve through this appearance of a downward spiral of fear-based hatred and come out stronger, happier, and healthier. We can live in peace with all people everywhere as one in the Great Spirit.

"Oh sure, the skeptics are saying, you can never put two opposing groups or tribes in a room and ask them to forgive each other. You cannot bring peoples together that have hated one another for centuries and say, 'Okay, guys, now it's time to love each other,' but I beg to differ," said Leonard. "What would life be like if we simply said, 'I forgive you? I love you. You are my brother or my sister and I wish for the fighting, dying and starvation to end. Can we please forgive one another and move on?'

"Just as an example," he said, "let's try this: I forgive the police and military for pretending to be Nazis. I forgive armies for the killing of innocent women and children. I forgive the government for acts of treason. I forgive corporations for taking advantage of less-educated people in Third World countries and starving their children. I forgive the Whites for suppressing Blacks, Hispanics, Natives, and Asians for hundreds of years. I forgive my spouse for debasing me. I forgive the rapist who took my life from me. I forgive my parents for not wanting me and not understanding how to raise a child. I forgive the teachers in my school that understood little more than control. I forgive my farther for raping my sister and beating my brothers and me on a daily basis. I forgive all those who have falsely accused me and attempted to damage my reputation.

"And while you're at it, one could say, 'I forgive myself for all the wrongdoings I have committed throughout all of my life to everyone, everywhere.' One could even say a short prayer and ask for forgiveness for the acts of violence or acts of omission one has committed in his or her own life experience towards all other people, animals, plants and trees."

"Whoops," he said, "that means taking responsibility seriously, now, doesn't it?"

"And what's the outcome we might expect? Well, why don't we all just do a little experiment starting today and find out? Find someone to forgive. Let them know they are forgiven and ask them to forgive one other person. Look at it this way, what have you got to lose? Your pride? Your manhood? Your woman's integrity? Nothing at all should stand in the way of the peace we could experience through forgiveness. If three people forgive three people and they forgive three others, there is no telling where it might lead. To Peace?" He asked.

Leonard said, "There is no higher purpose than love and if we can do this simple act we can, in fact, live in our highest and best realization of ourselves. There is no other way.

"Forgiveness. I'll start today, and why don't you join me? If you don't," he said, "I forgive you."

May 1990, Six Mile Hike Up to Rock Lake, Way Over West, Near Idaho

Chapter 5
When the Wind Died Down

Several years ago, I was involved in a project to help save the endangered mountain bluebird. The organization I created and managed, along with my former wife Pamela, was called *Project Bluebird*. Its mission was to help protect the endangered bluebird and bring it back in strong numbers from possible extinction. The mountain and western bluebird were near extinction, mostly due to poor environmental practices, especially the heavy use of pesticides near nesting areas, which are normally on fence lines near commercial farming operations. We financed our efforts by selling thousands of birdhouses made from recycled materials, which Pammy painted and decorated with wonderful designs. Due to our effort of providing luxury housing to the bluebirds and helping to change spraying practices, they have come back in big numbers. Why is this important, you might ask? Every pro-environmental action by Project Bluebird is a benefit to the entire environment.

Jay with Project Bluebird, 1993, Kalispell, MT

Leonard was the Executive Advisor for the organization and he was always on hand to give advice. Leonard believed all living things require respect and love. He believed no creature was greater than another, whether human or animal.

Respect for all life is the Native American way. Many years before we faced problems of pollution, overcrowding, extinction of animal and plant species, and other such problems, they knew that conservation and respect for our natural resources was the key to survival for everything on Earth.

Yes, the Natives killed to eat. The difference is that they *used* these resources to the fullest. Nothing was ever wasted. Every part of the animal sacrificed for food was used, including the meat, hide bone and guts. Our politicians who bicker and quarrel over how to conserve our resources and the environment would be well served to study the Native ways of using what we have to its fullest potential, eliminating waste and irresponsibility, and being good stewards of the earth.

My responsibilities for the Project Bluebird organization were rather full. I wore several hats within the organization, and at times I felt overwhelmed and exhausted.

One winter day I was in a meeting with the staff discussing plans, projects and programs for the organization. The staff was facing me in a half circle in my office, all positioned toward the widow behind me. I noticed they were completely distracted—not into the meeting at all. I asked what the heck was going on. Was I the only one interested in what we were talking about? They all laughed and said in unison, "Quick, Jay, turn around!" There it was, a Bald Eagle in the pasture across the street devouring a rodent it had just caught.

I said, "Great, now we can all get back to business."

After the meeting was over, Leonard came to my desk and said, "Jay, you need a break. Have you ever been winter camping?"

"Leonard, what are you talking about?" I asked. "It's the middle of February, 20 degrees below zero and, no, I have never been winter camping!"

"Good," Leonard replied, "Be ready about noon Friday. Have your big tent in your truck and all the rest of your gear. See you Friday!" and he was out the door before I could ask if he had lost his mind.

"Pammy, did you get all of that?" I asked. "Leonard actually thinks I'm going camping with him in the middle of winter."

Pammy replied, "And you should go, Jay."

"Have you lost your mind too?" I asked.

For two days I fretted, hoping Leonard had forgotten the whole thing and that by the time he came to the office it would just be back to business as usual. But on Friday morning Leonard arrived around ten a.m., Native time nine am, wearing a big, heavy jacket. "Got your gear together?" he asked.

"Oh, no," I replied.

"Jay, this is something you need to do as part of our connection. Let me help you get your things together," Leonard offered.

"Geez, Leonard, everything is out in the garage. The wind is blowing. And, what the heck is the temperature today?" I asked.

"Come on, let's get your things together," Leonard insisted.

I gave in. I bundled myself up in three layers of clothing and we packed the truck with enough food and coffee for three days. "Bye Pammy, I'm off to go winter camping…. Oh boy, isn't this going be fun?" I mumbled to myself.

Leonard said, "I heard that."

"Where are we off to?" I asked.

"Let's go over to the Kootenai River above Libby," Leonard replied. This is a big river in western Montana, near Idaho and just below Canada.

Leonard knew I loved to go fly fishing. "Bring your fishing gear?" he asked, "I hear there's some big ones over there."

"Yes, Leonard, I did, but I don't have a clue why. It's going to be way too cold to fish," I said.

White ice, black ice, whiteout snow, heading west out of Kalispell to Libby, which is normally two hour's drive, took us eight hours, on a white ice highway. We passed through Libby and headed north for a spot I had been to several times during the *normal* fishing season. "Okay, Leonard, we're here. Sure is nice and warm in the truck. Sure you want to get out?" I asked.

"Come on, let's get camp set up," Leonard said.

"Geez, Leonard, its friggin' cold out here," I said. The wind was howling. We looked like two guys from an old comedy movie in fast forward trying to set up my wall tent, which we finally managed to do after several attempts. I got the cook stove going and put on the coffee.

"Happy now, Leonard? Can we go home in the morning?" I pleaded.

Leonard replied, "Listen to that wind, boy. I'll bet every mountain bluebird in the neighborhood has headed for California. Listen, Jay. Listen to the wind through those trees. Where do you suppose the elk hide out during these storms? The bear—he's fast asleep. The geese have headed south, along with the trumpeter swan, but the deer and the elk have to stay. They don't travel as far as they used to. Kind of like my tribe," he said. "We used to head south out of this really cold stuff long ago when we were nomads. Ah, but golly," continued Leonard, "even the trees have a hard time in this weather. I'll bet you we hear some snap and fall while we are out here among them." Leonard loved nature and everything in it, even during a very cold winter.

We ate our dinner and turned in for the night. Except for having to get up to keep the fire burning, we had a pretty quiet night's sleep. We got up early in the morning just to have a look at how much snow we were going to have to deal with to be able to take a walk away from camp. "Not too bad," Leonard said, "It's only knee high," and let out a big laugh.

I just laughed with him. The wind and snow had stopped. I even tried fly-fishing for a minute. "Geez, Leonard, I can't get a cast off. The line won't make it through the guides! This is hysterical—I'm going back to bed," I said.

Leonard wanted to talk about the trees and the animals and about being out in nature. "Even during the cold of winter, there is nothing better," he said. "You know those people they call tree huggers?" he asked.

"Yes, Leonard, I think I'm one of them."

Leonard laughed. "Hell, we (Native People) were tree huggers long before anyone came along with that term." Looking out though the opening in the front of the tent, Leonard asked, "You see that huge tree out there, Jay? He's just as alive as you and I. If you go out there and hug him, you are going to feel his life. You will feel his vibration, and he will speak to you the same way the bear does. All you have to do is listen"!

"Man is a funny animal," Leonard said. "He thinks he is the only one with human life and feelings. This makes it easy for him to cut the trees and kill the bear. Man doesn't think they feel it or that they are missed by their relatives."

On day three, Leonard and I fooled around camp a little. We ate, we walked and we talked about man and nature. We talked a lot about the need for conservation and protection of the natural world. What the heck, I even got to where I didn't notice the temperature- too much!

In the afternoon I took off by myself and headed up a little knoll of a mountain just above the wide Kootenai River. I found a nice vista spot I have fished under several times before, but it didn't look the same. Everything was white. I cleared the snow away from the base of the trunk of a massive spruce tree, sat down, kicked the snow away from under my feet and got comfortable and quiet, as though I was there for a hunt- which we were not. I listened to the water running down the hill in the river. I noticed there was not a sound—not a bird chirping or an elk calling, even though I knew the rut season was far gone by. I thought to myself, "Gee, not a sound." No ice falling from the trees, no wind, no planes overhead, not a sound. After about twenty minutes, a thought came to me, "Gee, I haven't had a thought for several minutes now." I sat watching the river and observed clouds moving back in for what would most likely be the next storm. I just sat there listening to the quiet.

When I returned to camp, Leonard was in the tent reading a book. He let his glasses down on his nose, looked up and asked, "How was your walk?" I could barely speak of the experience. When I found the words, I told Leonard what I had felt. He said "Good. It's time to go home."

Chapter 6
It's Just Around the Bend

High above the Put-In Spot – This is World Class Fly-Fishing, Boys and Girls

In 1992, my very closest friend, Mahlon, showed up in Montana—well, he didn't actually just show up—I had known for months in advance that he and his new wife, Trisha, were planning a trip to Montana. I could hardly wait for them to arrive. Truth be told, I have never had much patience and the expectation of Mahlon coming to play with me in Montana was almost more than I could stand. This was a special friendship of long standing, and all too rare to find.

In our younger days, Mahlon and I had been all over the country together. We had hunted, fished, and partied our way through most of the states in North America from the 1960's on up through college and into adulthood, but we had never made it to Montana together. This would be his first trip to Big Sky Country.

Mahlon was a beautiful man in more ways than one. Yes, he was very good looking and many, many women were interested in him wherever we landed, but the truth is, he was only with four women his whole life. For Mahlon, it was love or nothing, and I always respected him for that. He was tall man and had blond hair down to his butt, and was a musician beyond comparison when it came to Flamenco guitar. He was also an outstanding clothing designer. But his personality, his beingness was also so beautiful. He loved people and everyone loved Mahlon.

For over two years, Mahlon had heard my stories about Leonard, Montana, and the fly-fishing, and he had to come to see it all for himself. He arrived at the Kalispell airport about midnight, and when he came through the terminal, I barely recognized him. He was pale and gaunt and had a yellowish tinge to his skin that I had seen before in seriously ill friends and relatives. After spending a few days with him, I felt sure he would soon be heading off to better hunting grounds, and as it turned out, not long after his visit to Montana, Mahlon passed away from a short but deadly bout with throat cancer—maybe a good reason for us all to quit smoking cigarettes.

Pammy and Mahlon were also very good friends. Mahlon knew Pammy before I met her, and as a mater of fact, he had invited me to a party at her house two years before Pammy and I finally met. I was not able to attend the party that night due to a cousin's wedding, but all turned out well, I'd say! Pammy and I cried together in our bedroom at the prospect of losing our good friend, and I told her many stories of our travels over four decades.

Up early on the third morning of their visit and just after coffee, Mahlon asked, "So, where is all this great fly-fishing you have been bragging about?"

"Okay buddy I'm going to start you out on what should be the climax of your trip," I said. "We are going to float the south fork of the Flathead River tomorrow. It's about an hour away from our place up toward Glacier National Park. You'll like it, trust me!"

I started to get the gear together and called Joe, my new Montana buddy, to ask what time we should meet up at Spotted Bear that afternoon. Spotted Bear was a 52-mile drive off the highway on a twisty, dusty, dirt road that paralleled the edge of the Bob Marshall and Great Bear Wildernesses. We agreed to meet up at five that afternoon, camp one night, and start the float the next morning. As soon as I hung up, the phone rang. "Jay, it's Leonard," Pammy said.

"Oh my! Great! I want you to meet him while you're here," I told Mahlon.

"Hey, Leonard, what's up?" I asked.

"Nothing, just thought Dee and I would take a ride over the mountain and come for a visit," he said.

"When?" I asked.

"Today, by golly," he replied. "We thought we would head out this morning."

"Oh geez, Leonard," I said, "my best friend is here from California and we're headed out the door for a float trip down the Flathead."

"Great!" he replied, "can I come along?"

"Hell yes," I said. "I want you guys to meet."

We made plans to meet Leonard at the entrance to Hungry Horse Reservoir and he would drive in the rest of the way with Mahlon and me. Pammy and Trisha would take Dee back to our house.

"Let's meet around two in the afternoon, Leonard. That's white man's time," I said, which to Leonard meant, "Be on time."

We began to make preparations for food and what-not. Don't ask what a what-not is, it's just something that exists in Montana, because everybody says it! And please don't ask what a what-not looks like because nobody really knows—it's just what-not!

Leonard and Dee arrived on time. We kissed the ladies goodbye and started our drive in to Spotted Bear Camp, not far from the headwaters of the Flathead, where we would put-into the river the following morning. When we arrived at the agreed-upon spot, Joe was already there and had a nice fire going. We fixed elk burgers from an elk that Joe had shot the previous fall and sat around camp telling jokes and listening to Leonard fiddle on the violin.

"Let's turn in and make it a great float in the morning," Joe said, and we all climbed into our sleeping bags.

"Don't let the bears bite," said Leonard.

"Good night Leonard," we replied.

We woke early to a magical morning in the forest with the smell of fresh dew on the ground. We stirred around camp for a bit, had a bite—there's nothing like bacon and eggs cooked over a hot fire in the woods, and of course, some of my coffee for Leonard and my buddies.

Joe said, "Let's have a float."

Just before we left, Leonard walked down the short slope to the water's edge and tied a tin can to a large pine tree with twine. We took two trucks out of camp, one to be used as a portage truck when the float was over to retrieve the carry truck, which carries all the gear and passengers up river to the put-in spot. The three of us went with Joe in his old beater Chevy truck to the put-in, along with the float boat and all of our gear. We carried the gear down the steep mountainside to the put-in spot just past Hell's Gorge, a place no fool would ever try to float through, although it has been done. From our vantage point, we could look up river and see the tail end of the gorge and hear the raging waters upstream in the canyon.

"Shit, no thanks!" said Joe, "not in this lifetime," and we all shook our heads in agreement.

It is difficult to describe the immense beauty of the place, the crystal clear water, the huge rock faces with trees growing right out them, and the air so fresh and so beautiful you could eat it. We saw elk, deer, moose, and even a griz, (grizzly bear) and there were thousands of hungry cutthroat trout, thank God. A cutthroat is the trophy of wild trout to many Western fly-fishermen because they are *wild* and brightly colored, with a bright red stripe just under the jaw gills.

From the put-in to the Spotted Bear campsite is only 14 miles, as a crow flies, but we were on twisty, sometimes fast and often slow sections of the south fork, and it was much more than 14 miles of floating.

We fished, we talked, and we laughed—we laughed a lot. And, might I add, we caught our fair share of east slope cutthroat. We made our way down to about the halfway point at Table Rock and got out of the raft to enjoy the sandwiches we had brought along from home. After lunch, Leonard made his way up a short knoll and I followed.

"Your friend is quite ill," he said.

"Yes, I know," I replied. "I can see that he is."

"He will not be here long, Jay," said Leonard, and I began to cry.

"Yes, I know, Leonard and I hate giving him up."

"What? Where is your faith, my boy?" asked Leonard. "How do you see this as giving him up? He will always be your friend and he will never give you up. He is headed for a transition. Instead of crying, you should give praise and thanksgiving for knowing such a beautiful man. Never give up your faith that he is your friend. He will always be your friend; this will never end. Faith, my boy, never give up your faith."

I thanked Leonard and felt a little better. We made our way back down the hill and there was

Mahlon's beautiful, smiling face. "This place is amazing," he said. "I will be back here one day."

I gave him a hug and said, "Yes, you will."

We all piled back into the raft and started the float back to camp. After about a mile or two, Joe said, "Whoa, its five o'clock and we aren't even halfway home. Let's start paddling a bit and see if we can make some time."

Shortly, a huge headwind came up and practically stopped us on the water.

"Gees, raft ain't moving much," I said.

Leonard leaned against the back of the raft and said, "Ha, have some faith. We'll get there."

After about five hours of struggle in the dark, I said to Joe, "Geez, it's got to be just around the bend."

After about twenty bends in the river and no sight of what looked like Spotted Bear, I said, "Geez, it's got be just around the bend."

Joe said, "If you say that one more time..."

A while later, Joe said, "Its one o'clock in the morning. I think we must have passed the camp."

Leonard said, "No, we didn't." He shot his flashlight up on the bank and said, "It's just around the bend." Two minutes later, he flashed the light on the tin can he tied on the tree the morning before. "Just a little faith," he smiled.

Leonard, Mahlon, and Pammy are gone from this place now, and I never give up my faith they are right here with me today.

Looking up at Sacred Heart Butte from Leonard's Place

Chapter 7
Late One Summer Afternoon

Late one summer afternoon, during one of the darkest times of my life, I was sitting on Leonard's porch east of the divide in northwest Montana, looking up at Heart Butte Mountain—usually a most welcome sight—but not that day. I was in total misery.

I was lonely, upset, and depressed. I had just lost my wife to cancer, and several of my closest friends and relatives had passed recently as well.

Leonard had taken notice of my mood. He said, "Its okay to feel what you are feeling, Jay."

I replied that I missed many loved ones and feared I might be next.

By way of reply, Leonard asked me to participate in a traditional Blackfeet journey of old. "Close your eyes and listen," said Leonard.

"Go, Jay, live with the Elk Clan high up in those mountains," Leonard said. "Be of the Elk Clan. Live with them and learn what you can from them."

When I arrived, I noticed the Elk Chief had all the best grass for himself and would not share it with the other members of his clan. He was a danger to his clan; he was selfish and greedy, and allowed all the other elk in the tribe to die of starvation. Leonard advised me that this evil needed to be confronted like any other evil and that I should slay the Elk Chief. I did this, but it was painful for me, and left me feeling even more lonely and dejected.

"Go, Jay, off to the west Mountains and be with the Bear Clan," Leonard directed. "Live with them and freely take what gifts they offer."

When I arrived, I noticed the Bear Chief had the all the females in the camp to himself. He had stolen all the female bears from the males of the clan, whom he feared and hated. He would not share the female bears with the males of the clan. He was cruel and angry most of the time; he beat the female bear and would not share his berries with them. All the male bears in the camp were cold and lonely. They had no love of their own, as all the female bears were possessed.

"This Bear Chief must be slain so all the other males in the clan can have their females back," proclaimed Leonard.

"But, the Bear is sacred and should not be harmed," I replied.

"Not when all he does demonstrates hate and destruction," Leonard said. "Kill him and give his skin to the bear females."

I killed him, and Leonard sent me to live with the Buffalo Clan on the plains.

I found the Buffalo Clan plentiful, but I was pained to see that the lead bull, Buffalo Chief, made all the other buffalo in the clan worship him and bring him all the best grass. He was lazy and would not lead the clan to new grass, but rather had them toil and do all the work for him. He allowed them only a very small portion of grass for their families.

"This bull must be destroyed!" Leonard cried. "Take his life, use his meat to feed yourself and the rest of the clan all winter, build a robe from his skin and a knife from his bones."

I did this, and Leonard told me to be off to the plains far to the east to live with the Coyote Clan.

The first thing I noticed was that the Coyote Chief was a thief and stole all the best fresh meat for himself. He would not share, even with his own family. Every coyote in the clan was starving. Even Coyote Chief's own daughters were hungry but could not hunt for themselves because they were too weak. The Coyote Chief had the very best den. His cave was lavish, warm and garish with decorations from his thievery.

"This Coyote Chief is evil," Leonard said, "and must be killed so all the other coyotes may live well and prosper. Kill him, feed his meat to the Coyote Clan and build a neck warmer from his hide."

I did this, and Leonard sent me to live with Antelope Clan, not too far away.

The Antelope Clan had been taught by their Chief to fear all the animals in all other clans. He told them to stay on the move and to run very quickly at any sign of danger. He was very hard on his clan. "Keep moving," he told them. "Stop only ever so briefly to feed and water. Dash at the first sign of trouble and danger. Don't seek a confrontation—run like hell and don't look back."

The trouble was the antelope of his clan were thin and full of fleas, because they could not take the time to bathe. They had to be on the move and be ready to "carry the mail," (a Native term which means to run very fast) at first sign of trouble. Antelope Chief was killing off his clan without even realizing it.

"Destroy this Antelope Chief or he will certainly kill off the entire clan," Leonard sang out. "Make a spear from his horns and feed the meat to your dog."

I did this, and Leonard advised, "With those wings of yours, take flight and fly among the Eagle Clan."

There were not many eagles in the Eagle Clan, and the ones I came upon were ignorant. They could not fish nor tear open the guts of dead animals. The Eagle Chief did not teach his clan. He encouraged laziness and recommended that the clan eat what the Owl and the Hawk Clans dropped off.

The Eagle Clan was dwindling in numbers, feeding on mostly foul meat that was not desired by the other bird clans. The clan was ignorant of what to eat and how to feed their young. The Eagle Chief was killing off his own clan by his ignorance.

"This Eagle Clan represents very old wisdom and the Eagle Chief must be slain so the other Eagles of the clan can remember who they are and return to their proud status. Kill this chief," Leonard said. "Bury him and never look upon him again. Go off and be with the Mouse Clan."

And I did.

The Mouse Clan was very busy, moving about, scurrying to do apparently nothing at all. They exhausted me. No one in the Mouse Clan had purpose or meaning in their life. The Mouse Chief had his clan rushing about to gather what every other clan had discarded. They picked up bits and pieces of what the other clans left behind, never having the whole of any particle. The Mouse Chief had instructed his clan to stay very busy gathering and collecting everything they could get their hands on, even if what they brought home had neither function nor usability.

"Just gather, and if what you bring home is not of any value to your family, sell it to another clan and make a handsome profit. Don't worry if it doesn't work or serves no purpose," the Chief advised. The Mouse Clan had grown very tired and weak from so much activity, but that did not matter. The Chief's greedy and covetous instructions had to be carried out at all costs—even if it meant killing off his own clan.

Leonard said, "The Mouse Chief creates too much clutter with all of his greed and sinfulness. Kill him and feed his meat to the Rat Clan. After the Mouse Chief's death, there will be no mourning." When I had done this, Leonard told me to go be with the Goose Clan.

The Goose Clan was very loyal to their families, traveled freely and ate good grain wherever they landed. The Goose Chief advised his clan to marry only once and to be the strength their mate required. "Share all you have with every other clan. Teach—but do not preach—love, peace, and joy. Be in your own strength and never disparage it. Allow others to be exactly who they are." The Goose Chief was immensely full of wisdom and encouraged the members of his clan to seek useful knowledge and fly high.

"Fly in great numbers, warn one another of danger. Drink only clean water. Eat until you are full and take no more. When your loved ones cry for you to go to them, do so and arrive with an open heart," he told them.

"Fly high and take notice of where you are at all times. Be aware there is only this moment. Take long walks daily, get rest, and enjoy your days with one another.

If one of the clan should become lost, the whole clan should go and find the missing one. Remember who you are and know where you came from."

Leonard advised me to take the Goose Chief's life, "Consume his meat. Allow his love to strengthen your body, free your mind, heal your soul and add everything you require into your life."

After the seventh Chief was killed, Leonard said, "Kill no more and return to life. Give thanks to the Creator."

I did, and mourned no more.

We do not fear death when we realize that it is not the end of life, but rather a part of it, and that there is death in some form every day; the challenge for many of us, is to simply experience it.

From my journey, I learned that death is actually the beginning of a new and perhaps better life. Instead of fearing death, we must learn to live life—fully, truly and honestly. Once we do this, death will not bring the hopelessness of loss, but rather the reward for what we have made of life, and the joy of memories filled with love rather than regret. "Fly high, use wisdom, and mourn no more," said Leonard. Live life. Don't worry about its beginning or ending.

Poster from the Famous 101 Ranch

Summer 1991: View from Picture Ridge to the China Wall

Chapter 8
The Story of Picture Ridge

As we have discussed, life is not made up of a few monumental events, but the day-to-day experiences we have are what really matters. What matters most are the important ones in our lives. How many days have you awakened, expecting that day's experiences were to be relatively uneventful in the grand scheme, and they ended up changing life as you knew it forever?

It was September, the beginning of fall, high up in the Bob Marshall Wilderness of northwest Montana. Leonard called to say, "Those Mountains are calling to me. How about an early season elk hunt before the snow gets too deep?"

"Sure," I said, let's go."

Leonard offered to get his horses and mules ready and asked me to pack my big wall tent, the cooking gear, and food for five or six days. "Let's meet at the end of the road at the Big Springs camp spot," he said. "You know, the one around the bend from Spotted Bear," said Leonard with a laugh. "We'll set up camp there and prepare the stock for the ride up the mountain to Picture Ridge."

The drive north is incredibly beautiful, as you head out of Kalispell, past Hungry Horse, just southwest of Glacier National Park. This is BIG country, with huge spruce and white pines. The drive on the dirt road to the campsite at Spotted Bear is 52 miles of dust, twists, and beautiful vistas of the South Fork Flathead River, waterfalls, and lush green forest.

Often, one can see bears, both black and griz. You can count on seeing deer. And during the harsh winter, if you go even a short distance off Highway Two, you'll see plenty of elk, which otherwise can be a considerable chore to find, especially during elk hunting season. They don't call them *Wapiti* for nothing. Their Indian name means *ghost of the forest.*

"Howdy Leonard, how was your trip over?" I asked. Leonard comes over from east of the divide, from Heart Butte, also known as Old Agency, the white man's name for the first settlement on the Blackfeet Reservation back in the late 1800s.

"Oh, by golly, it was a chore," Leonard replied. "The mules were kickin' up a storm in the trailer. Well, we're here. Got any coffee going?" he asked.

"No, but it'll only take a few minutes to put up." Leonard loves my coffee and to keep him hooked, I never gave up the recipe.

"Rain may be coming!" Leonard said. "Let's set up the wall tent down here, get these animals fed, and go to bed."

Weather anywhere near "The Bob", as the locals affectionately call the wilderness area, is totally unpredictable. The only way to know the weather for sure is to stick your head outside and see what it's doing. And, as they say in those parts, if you don't like it, wait five minutes 'cause it's bound to change.

We got ready to turn in after a hot cup of deer soup, some French bread, and a couple of pots of coffee. Back in those days, Leonard and I drank so much coffee it never kept us awake.

"What do you think this weather is going to do?" I asked Leonard.

"Who knows? Could be why them mules were so uppity. Maybe they know something we don't," Leonard replied. "We'll know in the morning. Good night."

Leonard woke me in the wee hours before the sun was up, "Geez Jay, what the heck is going on here?"

"What?" I asked.

Leonard replied, "Sounds like World War Three out there."

The rain and hail were coming down like huge stones, and the river was starting to gush.

"Leonard, its four o'clock in the morning. Go back to sleep."

"Who can sleep in this?" Leonard asked.

"I can," I said, "and that's what I'm about to do. Let's see what it looks like in the morning when we get up."

By sunrise the rain had become a light drizzle, and it wasn't all that cold. "What do you think, Leonard? Want to make the trip up the mountain to camp at Picture Ridge?"

"Well, we're here. We came all this way with all this gear, and at this time of year, that is where the elk are going be. What the hell? Let's get up there and see just how deep it snowed last night."

After about four hours of tying and retying packs on the mules, we were ready to start a twenty-five mile ride up to a spot we knew well, Picture Ridge. Handsome elk from this area have provided plenty of winter meat for hunters and their families, season after season. It's rough country, and not for the soft going or tenderfoot, as the less eager types of folks as they are often referred as in Northwest Montana.

The ride up is beautiful, although steep and rugged. We saw a few deer, which we chose not to take 'cause there is always time to take a deer in Montana'. We were after elk!

"Oh, by golly, it's starting to snow," Leonard said.

"Yeah, no kidding," I replied.

"Oh man, the wind is starting to blow good too," Leonard said.

"Let's get our butts up past the ridge, Leonard."

We cranked the horses and mules up over the hump and were on the ridge looking straight over to the China Wall and the Sun River about two thousand feet below.

"My God, Leonard, this is amazing!"

"Yep. Never tire of seeing it, do we?" Leonard replied. "Let's get across the ridge and to the flat spot and set up camp."

"Yeah, right," I replied.

The wind was howling and the horses were screaming as if to say "Get me the hell out of out of here!" We managed to set up camp, get the horses fed, cut some dead fall for firewood, and cook a pretty nice meal, complete with my coffee for Leonard. About midnight we were exhausted and ready to turn in.

"Let's get after them in the morning," Leonard said.

"Good night!" I replied.

"Ho emm, Leonard. It's ten-thirty."

"Ten-thirty what?" Leonard asked.

"In the morning! Think we missed the morning hunt?"

"Oh, geez, let's just go back to sleep then," Leonard replied.

Finally, about four o'clock that afternoon, Leonard and I got up to take a look and a long-awaited pee outside.

"Geez, it's still snowing, Leonard."

"Yep, visibility is about five yards. We didn't miss much, did we?" Leonard asked.

"Nope. Let's get the stock fed, have a quick bite, and go for a little walk about before it gets too dark," I said.

To cut to the point, and not bore you with everything we found to complain about, it snowed on us for four days and nights. By the fourth day, we actually had to dig our way out of the tent to feed the horses and mules and do our private business. Go for a hunt? Not!

"Man, Leonard, this just ain't letting up. What do you wanna do?"

"We better get out, while the getting is good," Leonard replied. "We'll try for a mid or late season hunt down lower in a couple of weeks, when these elk get driven down."

At first light, we packed up camp, packed the stock, and Leonard said, "Jay, come on over here a minute."

I thought to myself, "Leonard, I have only the deepest respect for you, but this is no time for an old Indian story."

"Yeah, Leonard, what's up?" I asked with hesitation.

"Well, we gotta think about this. You know as well as I do, Picture Ridge has been snowed on for five solid days. It's a hundred yards long and one foot wide. How are we going to find the trail so we don't end up at the bottom of the canyon?" There was a two thousand foot drop on either side!

"Hell, I don't know, Leonard. Our only other alternative is Inspiration Peak, and that's all shale and a twenty-five mile ride in the wrong direction, and then about a hundred and fifty miles drive back to base camp. We have to go out the way we came in. There is no other reasonable way out," I said.

Leonard agreed.

No sooner had we mounted up then it started to snow heavily. About forty minutes into the ride, to the start of the thin ridge, the wind started to howl.

"Hell, Leonard, there is no trail!" I screamed ahead.

I heard Leonard say, "Shit! These horses will find the way."

I could barely see Leonard ahead of me and could only make out the mule's tail he was pulling behind. As I hit the ridge, I dropped the reins and said, "It's up to you, horse. Get us off of this mountain."

I turned up my collar, drew down my hat, said my prayers, and gave the horse a nudge to go. Had one near-miss at the end of the trail, but...

Yes, we made it out of there. Hell, I'm telling the story. But it's not over. We had just a moment to thank our lucky stars and move on because the storm was blowing. Halfway down the switchback mountain, the weather let up some and visibility was good.

"Leonard, look! There they are!"

A small heard of elk was on the side of the mountain, just northeast of our position.

"Ease on off. Let's take 'em," Leonard said.

"Okay, Leonard," I replied, "but remember, even if we get a clean shot and they go down quick, we still have to get 'em out of here!"

"You're right," Leonard said, "Let's take just one and we'll share the meat for our families."

"There they are, Leonard. You have a cow tag. What do you want to do, wait for the bull to show or take home some meat?" I asked.

"Bang!" It's decided. We are taking home meat.

"Clean shot, Leonard," I said. "She went down well." When we got to the beautiful animal, lying dead on the side of a small hill, Leonard knelt down, took off his hat and said, "Thank you Creator, thank you Great Spirit, you have supplied us well. This meat will strengthen our bodies, free our minds, and lift our spirits. Thank you Creator for this meat. Thank you for the hide to make a coat. Thank you for the spoils we will not consume but feed to our pets. Thank you for the innards we will leave for the bears, the birds and rodents. This is a good day to eat the heart." And he cut it out and gave praise and thanksgiving again and again as we sat there and ate the raw heart.

"Thank you, oh Great One, Grandfather, thank you". This heart builds our love for our families and gives us compassion for those with no heart for understanding. It gives us the wisdom to love the heartless," said Leonard. "Praise to the Creator!" he cried. "We have taken this great beast and we love her."

To the elk he said, "Thank you for giving us your life to teach us this love and to feed our hungry bodies."

We divided up the carcass to pack on the mules and without speaking made our way off the mountain of Picture Ridge. Occasionally some our best conversations were when Leonard and I didn't talk at all.

Chapter 9
She Has Arrived

One day Leonard came to me at my spot on the Res down on Two Medicine River. He had a guided message of peace, calming, and love, one that means very much to me. I hope it will find a way into your heart as well.

"Quiet and calm your mind, my son," Leonard said. "Come with me on a trip, eat these herbs, close your eyes, and allow yourself the freedom to quiet your mind. Let us rise above this troubled place to be with the Great One. We will hear his words." (In Native terms, the Great One is a he; no debasement of the feminine is intended- that is just the way of The People.) They speak of a higher power as 'he.' "His words will come and you will know the peace you seek. Let us rise to the mountains and above into the clouds and forget for just a moment who we think we are and allow the Great One to teach us of our true identity."

We lay quietly together on the grass for about twenty or thirty minutes, and Leonard began to chant and cry, "Who is this boy who knew great love and now lives in this place alone and in so much pain?"

Words came from Leonard like a fast-flowing river, and I had to listen intently to get all the meaning so I could absorb the truth in the meaning and his teaching. *"He who is One With Heart Foolishly Wide Open,"* my given Native name, *"does not discern well. He loves freely and foolishly and does not see evil until stung by her bite. He has come to lose many loved ones: wife, family, close friends, and he does not understand the meaning in their passing. He only feels the loss and even in his communion with his loved ones' spirits, he still depends on their flesh existence for his happiness."*

Spirit, through Leonard, went on to say, *"He has had plenty of time to see who he is and to understand the needs of others. He has come to know the importance of his service on this place we call Earth. He has good prosperity, fun, music, dance, excessive food, and fest. Remind him to give thanksgiving each day and to let go of all fear and anger. This might be a challenge for him, but it is very important for his next steps on your plane.*

"This spirit you call Jay requires the love of a good woman. He has learned that a woman will give him what he gives, just as the world gives back to him what he gives and presents to it. He has learned that to gain respect, he must give it. He has found her faithfulness resides in his own. Caring is in his hands.

Sharing of real, purposeful communication lies in his willingness. He must be the teacher and the student.

"In this modern time she has knowledge to share, and his wholehearted participation in her teachings will reap him many rewards. Quiet him. Have him lay on the beach of a quiet lake, and as the water flows over his body from his feet to his head like golden rays of sunshine, slowly in rhythmic pace, he becomes free to be the one he lays next to. Have him keep his eyes on me as she appears, and they will never die, no, only be held together in the bliss of shared purity and good works. He will know she is real based on his own knowledge of the tunes of the love flute. When he hears this sound, he knows reality. Have him let go.

"Go, Jay, up to the mountain. Take with you your most valued possession, and burn it. Pray, fast, sweat and scream, wash your face daily in the cold stream, build a sweat lodge, go into it for three days, fast, save for water only, return to the top of the mountain, stand strong, raise your arms out to your sides, turn to the east. She has arrived. In unison, you realize there is no greater power than love. Write it."

IT'S IN HER EYES WHEN SHE ARRIVES

When she arrives
I will know her
because I have known
her for a very long time

She will blow in like
a breath of fresh air

The wings on her back will
carry the fragrance of the

Goddess

Her smile will light the world
And heal my very soul

Her touch will free me
from my body

I then will know freedom
Her words will give sight to
the blind

Planet Earth will
come to recognize greatness
in witness of
great love

Her breath will bring life

where there once was only
suffering

Love, Peace and Joy in an instant
become reality

I will know her when she arrives
After all, just look into her eyes

Leonard awoke from his half sleep.

"Go now," he said, "and be sad no more. The tribe is always with you, and the message of love has come to you. The Great Spirit's powers bring you great love. You have known great love and will again one day."

We rose to our feet and chanted together and danced the Friendship Dance. We fixed a fine meal and Leonard's favorite coffee, and I drove off the reservation at midnight with a greater hope, a greater respect for my wise friend and a better understanding of how sometimes a time of suffering can be the only path to healing and later love, joy and peace.

Flathead Music Festival 1993

Chapter 10
Speak with Intention

Pammy, my beloved late wife of 24 years, and I were getting ready for a long-awaited trip to the Flathead Music Festival, a weeklong music festival held in the Flathead Valley of northwestern Montana. Leonard was to be playing. He was a world-class fiddle player and his "thing" was bluegrass. When he played his violin, he smiled and looked proud. It was more than a love of the old music; it was as much a respect for tradition and all it symbolized. Leonard loved to practice and pass on the traditions of music, knowledge of nature and the skills of using the earth to provide for your family's needs.

The festival, held in Whitefish, Kalispell and Big Fork, Montana, is one of the state's biggest tourist draws. People come from all over the world to listen, dance, and have a plain good old time. They come to hear the very best in rock, jazz, classical, blues, reggae, and bluegrass music. The festival is held in June, coming out of a long, wet, spring, and most of the locals look forward to it. It helps to lighten things up and ushers everyone, mentally, into summer.

Pammy and I knew for a long time ahead of the event that Leonard would be playing at the festival with a group he had put together. Waiting all winter and spring for June to come was like waiting for ice cream in a long line that barely seems to crawl along. We planned all winter and helped make arrangements for friends and family to rendezvous at a popular campground just outside of Leonard's venue in Kalispell. We had to book our campsite several months in advance, as they go quickly, and we knew we were going to need a huge spot. We landed a really cool site, right on the middle fork of the Flathead River, in a well-kept campground with beautiful, huge pine trees and grand, rolling grass fields. They even had hot showers. The only drawback in the summer are the mosquitoes, thicker than fog as the locals like to say.

Pammy and I and a few of our local friends got to the campground a few days before the kickoff of the week's event to set up what we called the Hospitality Refuge. It was a massive canvas tent—an older, smaller version of a big circus tent. Inside we hung all kinds of colorful and crazy fabrics that Pammy had collected, along with hundreds of throw pillows and carpets from thrift shops. We had all kinds of food and beverages to put out for our guests.

We were set for a huge party, because in addition to Leonard's huge family and our friends in the area, other musician friends were welcome to invite their friends to join our camp, not to mention the drop-ins no one would even know.

Just as people started to arrive, a friend of ours brought in a professional sound system so we could help get people in the mood and in the groove. I could tell it was going to be a sleepless week. Pammy and I were really into the arts, and we outdid ourselves to set up the camp. And it was a big hit. All week long people arrived and let us know they had heard of the camp at one of the festival's events and that they just had to come see it. We had drop-ins, we had people playing music, we had sleepovers and we even had a few folks that passed out due to just a little too much refreshment in very hot weather.

After Leonard's performance, several of his fans stopped by to say congratulations and let him know how much they appreciated his music. It was nearing the end of a long, joyful week of music, dance, and feasting. Around five o'clock in the morning, four people, two men and two women, we had not met before showed up at the tent. I was out having a smoke and a cup of coffee, and Leonard was just retuning after an early morning stroll. The foursome was obviously a little weary from the long event and we could tell they hadn't had much sleep.

They were in awe of the tent, the art, and decorations, and they wanted to share their appreciation and thank us for putting it up. "Come in, let's sit a while," Leonard and I invited them in. People were asleep all over the place and we spoke in a hushed tone.

As we sat together in one side of the tent away from the folks who were still asleep, we began a conversation. Each of us participated in turn. Each speaker got to hold the rock, so to speak (no rock was actually in place—this is just the Native way of saying they had the floor), and when he or she was finished speaking, passed the rock (so to speak) to the next person. To pass the rock in Native terms means that whoever is holding a small stone gets to speak as long as he or she wishes and gets to say whatever is on her or his mind and gets to communicate anything on any subject.

As we sat informally in a semi-circle, we spoke about the event, the music, the people, the costumes, and the art of it all. We told the stories of our lives, where we had been, what we were up to and where we thought we might be headed. Each person spoke without interruption. No projections or judgments were placed on the speakers. They were allowed to speak their truth. Each spoke deeply from the heart and was honored for what they had to say. No one was judged or put down in any way. No one led the conversation, no one was cut off, each person listened to the other and every person was acknowledged for what they had to say.

Leonard and I shared this sort of magical moment in Paradise for several hours with the foursome that had showed up. We exchanged massages, made breakfast together, and tossed in a little prayer over our meal. As we ate, we shared stories of great food and travel. We savored every bite.

After breakfast, the musicians of this small group played a little music and we drummed together. But, for me, what was so remarkable was the style of communication, the truth, and the honesty. Each person in our small group spoke intently, listened intently, and was honored for what he or she had to say.

The morning came to an end around two in the afternoon as some of us needed to sleep and others had to be off to the next life event.

"Leonard," I asked, "Have you ever experienced anything so beautiful?"

"We had a fine way of counsel," he replied.

I was not familiar with that term so I asked, "What is the way of counsel?"

Leonard said, "For thousands of years, The People have had what we call intentional communication, where each person in a circle is allowed to speak and share what is on his or her mind, whether it is war, hunting, or the inclusion of a newcomer. No matter what the topic, each person is allowed to speak from the heart and say exactly what they wish. No one would ever consider interrupting the speaker and starting a new topic until the original speaker was finished and no topic was restricted because of someone's pre-conceived notion of good or bad. The circle was never broken until all were complete."

He explained that in the traditional way, no one could leave the circle for any reason, as that would break the bond and disrupt the energy of the meeting, for whatever purpose the counsel or circle was formed. Leonard went on to say that he enjoyed the day's events very much himself and that he believed all disputes and most of all wars could be ended with this style of communication.

"Speaking from the heart is easy once one becomes familiar with it and is allowed to do so," he said. "People everywhere could get exactly what you got today, Jay, if only they would allow the speaker to express his or her own truth and did not put too much value or judgment on the thoughts or words conveyed. In reaching an understanding with other humans, this is the only way.

"Speak intentionally, speak from your heart and let your words be heard. Listen very carefully as if your life hinged on the other person's words.

"We sometimes have to learn how to speak from our hearts," said Leonard. "Many of us spend our lives speaking the way we believe others want us to. We speak to please our parents, our peers, our lovers, and sometimes our children. Often, we have spoken for others' benefits for so long that we lose what we need to express, even within ourselves.

"Can we be honest when we are not happy with a particular human relationship? Can we be honest when our work is unfulfilling to us? Can we be honest when our belief system is challenged? Can we speak of it openly and honestly and be understood?" asked Leonard.

"I challenge you, my friend, to find what you feel and what you think and what you want and what you need—and then to express it, peacefully, from your heart," said Leonard. "Yes, it may be different from what those around us want, think, need, or feel. It may even be contradictory. But you must know and speak your truth, because it is your truth that will set you free. And when you are free, my boy, you can free others.

"As with forgiveness, this will be hard, especially at first. But if those in your life are of true love, these differences will be a path to learning about each other and learning to accept each other. Always speak from the heart and listen intently," said Leonard.

"Find your counsel circle. Express yourself. Find the truth and be set free. Then set your mind to help others become free. Speak your truth and listen well," said Leonard.

Blackfeet War Counsel By Charles M. Russell—

World Famous Shot of Lake St. Mary, Glacier National Park

Chapter 11
The Ways of Nature

Delivered to me through Leonard about the things of nature and the spirit world we call home:

"Look here my son; do you see the way the fire burns in a circular motion?

"So it is with all things in Nature, even you and I. We are here and then we are not. We are there only for a little while, and then we are elsewhere, forever moving in the four directions of the fire circle.

"There is no other way. Everything is in one place for only a moment in time. It cannot stand still.

That is what made The People nomads for many thousands of years.

"We are one with the fire, the sun, the earth, the water, and the air. They are in constant motion. We are that. There is no other way.

"We are like birds in flight, moving in one direction or another with only one thing in mind—to survive. There is no other way. It is our Nature.

"It is in that mountain. Watch and listen to her very carefully. Sit quietly. Do not speak of her. Observe her. Hear her. It is all Nature. Sing the Nature song and dance with her. She is a wonderful partner. It is her nature.

"Hear the song of the flute and you hear my truth. Walk the way of the Red Path and you will see. Walk the way of the bear and you will see there is no difference. It is nature, and there is no other way.

"When the drum song plays and we dance, we imitate the animal world, and in our dance of the animal world, our nature is revealed. There is no other way.

"When the woman of your dreams hears your song of the flute, she will come to you. There is no other way. It is her nature. Only the natural world can take man and woman by the hand and show them the way to walk.

"When you arrive at the mountaintop, you do not arrive there by riches, you arrive there by heart. There is no other way. It is Nature.

"When your brother calls out to you to come to be by his side, you must go. There is no other way. It is his nature to request you to be there and yours to respond. You must go. There is no other way.

"The natural world holds all the answers. It is in the sweat lodge, the dance, drum, and song. It is in the trees and the running water. It is our nature to hear the words, to hear the message of love or war, of fleeing or standing still. There is no other way.

"Men and women can walk this earth together, but without Nature, there is no way to hear or see the Creator, and He may not speak to them at all if not through Nature. There is no other way.

"My son, everywhere you go, there is Nature. Look all around you as you walk. As you speak from the heart, notice Nature. There is no other way. Walk barefoot on the Earth every day.

"Hear the elk cry at night. It is his nature. Observe the coyote dance. Hear the song he sings to his brothers. There is no other way.

"When you consume the herb, know from where it came. It came the only way it could, through Nature. There is no other way.

"Listen as you have before. It is in the wind, it is in the sun, moon, stars, and planet Earth, in the very soil you love so much. Nature is crying out to you, 'Hear me, hear me!' There is no other way.

"Nature holds all lessons for you every day. Will you play? Will you stand still? Will you listen? Is there any other way? Nature is in you now. Go be in her.

"Look to the East, and the lessons of new beginnings. Turn to the West, as the sun sets and brings a new rest. Face up to the North and find a time to be still. Gaze down upon the South and allow the healing that you require. The time has come to stay and experience. It is nature. There is no other way.

"It is all here for your asking without the slightest struggle. It's all here for you now, and it is free. It is Nature.

"Give thanks and praises to the Creator. It is in the circle of Nature, and it is your path to look after her. There is no other way."

Leonard often spoke of Nature and the importance of listening, to hear her speak. He taught me to become silent and conscious of Mother Earth's needs and to protect and love her. "What you give her, she will give back to you a thousand times," Leonard said. "It is in her nature; there is no other way."

On one occasion, I said to Leonard, "There is so much oil, gold, silver, and oil up in those mountains. Why doesn't the tribe harvest some?"

"Because we like it right where it is Jay," he replied. "It is in our nature."

"Be in Nature," he pleaded. "Be with her daily. There is no other way."

Jay at (in) Two Medicine Lake—Fly-Fishing, 1994

Leonard also taught me that we must use our natural resources intelligently and look into our own hearts for guidance and to love our Nature.

"We live in a world," he said, "that is consumed by consumption." He believed that general Western culture couldn't grasp the concept of conservation because we spend every minute of every day gathering in order to spend. We work and then we spend more than we earn. We are given and use more than we've got. Get more, more, more—spend more, more, more. "That is not in our Nature," said Leonard.

Leonard owned very little, and he believed that we need to learn what many who suffered through the Great Depression and other human difficulties had to learn—that if we spend it all, it will be gone. "Some things," he said, "are just not replaceable, or will take many, many years to recover as in Nature." Yes, the Native Americans take what they need to use from the earth where they live. The difference is that their culture doesn't strip away what isn't needed or cannot be replaced.

Leonard said, "We need to shift our focus in order to survive and prosper. It is in our Nature to do so. It is a must," he said. "We need to be concerned about what we *need* rather than what we *want*. We have to focus on what we and our children will need in the future, and that future is now. Instead of *I, ME, Mine, and NOW,* we need to restrain ourselves so there will be Nature and a future for the ones who follow us." Love Nature; there is no other way!

Ghost Lake: Just off the Cut-Across Road on the Res, a Couple of Miles above Leonard's Place

*The Lodge Down in the Flats on Two Medicine River,
on the Res*

Chapter 12
The Sacred Sweat Lodge

There are secrets and mysteries to the sweat lodge that I am not allowed to reveal based on my sacred promises never to talk about them.

Each one of us has our own experience of miracles performed in the sweat lodge, and I'm certain your accounts will be sacred to you one day and will not be shared with anyone lightly.

Without revealing any secrets, here is just one of many such accounts of my time in the sacred sweat lodge.

Experiences such as this come not nearly often enough in our lives. You will see and know when you need one, and it is your responsibility to arrange it, to seek an accidental miracle. Life will not usually deal you everything you need. It is way too easy to make excuses like, "I don't have time," "It's too hard," or "Where would I find something like that?" But if you are truly seeking the path to fulfillment, freedom from the past, knowledge of yourself, the answers to life, and the ultimate unfoldment of your soul, you will find the time and the meeting place will come. You will make the time, and you will discover that it is time well spent, as I did with Leonard on so many occasions.

"I have a terrible headache, Leonard," I was whining. "This heat is getting to me and I have a massive headache going on." It was the hottest August I can remember! In these parts of Montana, we have winter. Sometimes we have August; this was one of those years.

Leonard said, "Time for a sweat." In Native life, almost any time is a good time for a sweat, a smoke, a dance, or a chant song.

The sweat lodge is one of the traditional ways of healing mind, body, and soul, and is always taken quite seriously. As a matter of fact, a person who does not approach it in reverence would not be welcome nor would a shaman avail himself for treatment and ask one to cross the line to come into the sweat lodge. Crossing the line is a time of reverence for ceremony, and one only does this at the right time. A woman must never cross the line during her moon cycle; this is considered very bad luck.

The sweat lodge is similar to the experience of quiet time, only it involves a physical purging in addition to mere reflection. It is a more active pursuit, but produces an after-effect of having been reborn and refreshed. As with the tribal commune, it combines the experience of coming together for self-examination and cleansing of what we have built up in our bodies, hearts, minds, and spirits as we walk through a convoluted world and provides a time to let go of the world for a short period of time.

Come Into the Lodge in Reverence and Silence

"Time to let go of the world. Let's go into the sweat lodge. Your head problems will be left there," Leonard said.

The sweat lodge in the Blackfeet Nation is a small half-dome; one has to kneel to go in. The body of the lodge is made from bent willow and is covered in either canvas or deer hides. Occasionally old rugs are used, but that is not tradition in the Blackfeet Nation.

The lodge usually holds up to six or eight people, but it can be only two if it is a ceremony, sacrifice, or ritual one is setting out to do. River rock (28 in total) is heated to a very high temperature outside the lodge, and in the traditional way, the rocks are passed in by a female virgin of the tribe using tree branches, as the rocks must be pure. The hot rocks are placed in the center of the lodge, and a mixture of water and herbs is poured over them. The opening to the sweat lodge or the door must *always* face east; there is no other acceptable direction, there is no other way! East represents new beginnings, the sunrise, mother's warmth, and healing.

There is always a leader or a shaman in the lodge, and he directs how the sweat will be run and its designated time. In other words, he decides how long we are to stay in the very dark, very hot lodge. Participants are encouraged to stay in the lodge for the entire duration of the sweat, and not to break the circle. The circle is of supreme importance to the Nation People, and we believe that if the circle had not been broken, we would not have lost our land and sacred buffalo.

The lodge is normally built near cold running water so when it is time to come out, we can dive into a lake or stream. Occasionally the sweat will go on for several days. We enter the lodge as a group and depart together, we take long walks in silence, we rest, we fast, save for water, and we sweat in a harmonious group.

Treatment is often performed to assist in the overcoming of an ailment, disease, discomfort, or nagging headache, such as the one I went in with.

Physical complaints are not the only reason for a sweat. On the contrary, we sweat to aid in our discovery, we sweat to help elevate ourselves to a place of desired strength and to achieve abilities. We sweat out the devil, we sweat in remembrance, and we sweat to clean impurities, both physical and mental, out of our bodies.

Herbs are always used in our sweats, and the ones utilized vary based on our particular desire and circumstance. Mugwort, Willowbark, and Chaparral are just a few examples. Herbs are used in many ways and are applied as part of the ceremony. They are breathed in as steam over hot rocks, they are eaten, they are boiled and drunk as tea, they are bathed in, they are taken in through the anus, and they are spanked or beaten into the skin with branches and leaves.

Some herbs make one feel terrible for a short period of time. This is expected. One will experience deep heaves, hot and cold sweats, deep pain and diarrhea. But it all passes, and one is encouraged to keep up one's courage and allow this process to take place. If you can't, you shouldn't be there in the first place. That is law.

Leonard had gotten word of a ritual sweat about to take place down in the flats at the east end of the Res, near a flat spot on the Two Medicine River—near desert country.

"Come; let us go into the sweat lodge. There is an elder running the lodge today, and he will be very happy to see you," Leonard said.

We approached the lower flatlands of Two Medicine River, which twists and turns its way down through what is the desert land off the reservation. Great for fly-fishing, but that was not our purpose this time. When we arrived, I could see about four or five naked old men wandering around a makeshift camp and gathering covers to go over the sweat lodge. The fire was already burning very hot, and the rocks were turning white from the coals. The camp was quiet, with the exception of warm greetings when we arrived, and it remained that way. The oldest member of the group, Earl, a small but hugely respected shaman, came over to greet me and said, "Good day for a sweat." He laughed, turned, and walked towards the lodge signaling for the rest of us to follow. We did, and before I knew it, I was in a very small space with six naked, worldly, old gentlemen, and the rocks began to come in. I recognized most of the members of the sweat from family gatherings and pow-wows.

Each had a reason for being there, and Earl asked us to state our purpose for being at the lodge that day. He asked each of us not to be concerned with the other members' purpose for their sweat. He said that was his job, and we all laughed out loud. Each man told his story, and each man was allowed to speak completely until done. It was informal, yet guided. We were allowed to pour out whatever we wanted to say, and Earl listened and acknowledged us completely. When we had all spoken, Earl started the singing and chanting that we would all follow in and participate with. These rounds of singing are done in fours and sevens, until twenty eight is reached and then start over.

Leonard noticed I was tense and asked me to just relax into it and allow whatever was to happen in the sweat lodge to happen or not. "Try not to expect too much," Leonard said.

Earl had herbs for each of us to ingest. He brought plenty of water for drinking and pouring over the hot rocks. He said he wouldn't let us suffer too much and we could go out for a pee and "what-not" if we wanted to. We were all comfortable, near as I could tell. From the glow of the rocks; faces looked cheerful.

Earl then began to move quietly and slowly around the lodge and touch each man. Some replied with a laugh, some with a cry, and one with a scream. Earl's movements and touching and caressing went on for what seemed liked several hours. The young lady outside of the lodge continued to send in hot rocks the entire time.

It was extremely hot. Each man washed his face several times with water that was brought in for us. The chanting, praying, and singing went on for several more hours. We were all exhausted and could barely stay awake, which is required. I was starting to fear I would not be able to stand it much longer and thought about a fast move to the door. Every now and then, I could feel Leonard's reassuring hand patting me on the knee as if to say, "It's okay kid, you'll make it."

Suddenly Earl said, "It is done!" We were finished with the sweat and allowed to go outside to cool off.

"Gee, my headache is gone, and I feel great," I said. Each man had something to say about the experience that had taken just over forty-eight hours with eight breaks in between intense HOT sessions.

What I witnessed in the lodge is very private, but I can tell you this: I saw things you'd think you would never see without the use of hallucinogenics. While the things I saw are secret, they are also very real.

All Leonard had to say was, "Nice sweat, eh? Let's go eat."

One day you will experience a sweat lodge, and my prayer and hope for you is that it is traditional and authentic and that you have someone by your side to pat you on the knee as if to say, "It's okay; you'll make it."

Leonard is gone from his body now, but every now and then I can feel him say, "It's okay Jay, you'll make it."

Jay and White Buffalo Speaks

Public Pow-Wow, 1997, Browning MT

Chapter 13
Come into Sacred Ceremony

Leonard said, "One day all people everywhere will come to know who they are. They will realize their own strength and power and be able to give loving service through their newfound knowledge and personal power."

He said that people already know this and that they either mask this inner wisdom or have somehow managed to forget who they truly are. "People act in funny ways when they are not being their true selves," he said and laughed out loud.

Leonard said that we are all leaders, writers, and artists; we are all mothers and fathers, teachers and healers. To Leonard there was nothing more important than people knowing who they are and what their true calling, or purpose for life, is.

"Come into scared ceremony," Leonard called. "Retrieve your soul, and never be shrouded in mystery again. Carry with you a hand drum, a shaker, sage, and a gift offering.

"Deep in those mountains, there is a valley. It has been sacred to our people for thousands of years and holds great medicine power unknown to most. Some of your people may not even recognize the power as they sit on this land," he said.

"Walk in, come to sacred ceremony in reverence and silence as you approach this valley. Ask the ancestors' permission to be there. Give praise and thanksgiving to the Creator for providing such a wondrous place. Take with you a valued possession and offer it as a sacred gift. Build an altar and chant a prayer. It does not matter in what language," Leonard said. "The Creator hears all languages.

"As you near the center of the valley, find your spot or the place you feel most comfortable, lay a blanket, and sit. Quiet your mind. Do not speak until it is time. Call in the ancestors and the great ones to be at your side and welcome their presence. Sit quietly for as long as you can. Light the sage, and with its smoke, bless this place, the surroundings, yourself, and whoever entered with you.

"Drum the drum song, chant and sing, and allow the Great Spirit to take over sacred ceremony. Allow Him to do the talking through you as you ask, 'Who am I?' It does not matter if you are unsure of the words that come, let them come. Dance, sing, and chant. If you have located running water and it is nearby, use your hands to scoop up the water to wash your face and head. Ask for purification. Continue to wash until you are cleansed. Continue. Allow the words to come. Be not concerned about whose words they are; be not concerned about your brain or any other apparent distraction, and simply ask.

"Now, ask again, 'Who am I? Who am I? What is my reason for being here?' Allow the great one to speak and you *listen*," Leonard advised.

"Some may need to go into the sweat lodge to help find these answers. Others may need to fast for several days. Some may need to climb the sacred mountain and stay on top for a week or more. Others will find it necessary to live the teepee life alone for an entire year to discover who they are and why they are here. No one is exempt from knowing these answers," said Leonard. "Money will not buy the desired result, drugs will only mask the way, and many therapists are of no value. Only the Great One can help reveal this and He does so through sacred ceremony.

"The only way for one to know is to ask, look, and be silent.

"Sacred ceremony is for anyone who chooses to know. It is not for the coward, for once one knows who they are and their reason for being, they will find they must take action in their lives and this may require drastic changes. This is not an easy way and the lazy will not attempt this path at all," he said.

"Come into sacred ceremony," Leonard called, "all the answers will be revealed there."

"This is not a once in a lifetime action. All mysteries are not revealed all at one time. No," Leonard said, "it is continuous. It is a process for your full development as a human being here in this place and the unfoldment of your soul. It takes patience and persistence. Remember this," he continued, "just when you think you have gone as far as you can and you're just too tired to go on and feel like giving up, that is when the mysteries will reveal themselves to you. There are many mysteries that will unfold during ceremony, and that is what makes this a process a lifelong journey."

Leonard said, "Once I had a young man come to me crying, 'I am going insane, Leonard, what do I do?' I replied, 'Dive deep into the pool of insanity. That is the only way for you to transcend it. That is your ceremony. There is no other way.'

"To walk the Red Path takes courage and determination. Never take the weak or half-hearted into sacred ceremony; you will only waste your energy," said Leonard.

"When one comes out of ceremony with newfound knowledge, they often cry in gratitude and want to offer a gift to the leader of ceremony. If you lead, never turn down the gift; you would only take away their appreciation and accomplishments," said Leonard. "For now they know who they are and know they know their path. Now they can fully love themselves and their neighbors. No one has told them this. No unwanted advice was given; no special training was required. Their own knowing and willingness to do ceremony has given them the knowledge that so many crave and no one can ever take that away.

"Never go into sacred ceremony lightheartedly," he insisted, "You can only enter with reverence, in silence, and with appreciation in your heart and love for the Great One."

Leonard could not stress enough the respect we must demonstrate for sacred ceremony and the appreciation we must show. To always praise the Creator and give thanks in deep appreciation is of paramount importance to The People of the Blackfeet Nation.

In a casual world, we no longer approach things with the reverence they deserve. Are we afraid of being serious? "Perhaps," said Leonard. Maybe we would be well served to ponder the seriousness of our lives, to focus on our health, our path and the welfare of others. Laughter, it is said, is the best medicine, and no one enjoyed a good laugh more than Leonard. But he was not afraid to give any situation the reverence it called for. "It is basic human respect," he said, "there is no other way."

Leonard said, "They may take our land, they may destroy my body, but they can never take away my real life and knowing who I am."

Leonard was a great man, huge in spirit, quiet in demeanor and a pure joy to be with. And still is very much today.

Chief Mountain, Named after Leonard's Grandfather

Chapter 14
He Came and I am Healed

Ho. Even in what appears to be a dark experience, there is light, there is teaching, there is healing. I have found that if we listen, we have the ability to heal ourselves. With the help and direction of the Great Spirit, we are healed. Aho.

One day when Leonard and I were walking in the hills on the Res just above his property talking about healing he said, "I think The Great Spirit is always ready for us—but sometimes he wants us to be here on earth and to serve our purpose before we move on."

There came a time in my life when I felt overwhelming fear and anxiety. It came over me like a tidal wave with much power and force and caused me to look, to look deeply, to look like I have never done before, and to look so deeply that a major change was destined to happen.

"Leonard," I asked, "are we always healed when we ask? Are there requirements for our healing? How is it that some bad people are healed and some good people are not?"

He replied, "When we quiet ourselves and allow healing, it will always come. Good and bad, well that just sort of works itself out. It's a deep subject and has to do with how we look at life, people, and things. People manage to see life with their own eyes well, and not so well with the eyes of their friends. But we can all allow a healing," said Leonard.

"Leonard," I said, "I have been diagnosed with a life-threatening illness, and I'm afraid. I'm not ready to give up this body, this life, or this journey yet. I do not feel ready to leave or to go be with elders of the tribe, not just yet," I said.

"Relax, relax, relax," Leonard advised me. "Relax in the Great One. He will guide you and show you the way. Relax Jay. Ask for the guidance you require."

Leonard asked me to chant with him for several days and to rest. "Get plenty of rest for that stressed body of yours, drink plenty of good, clean water, chant and pray, and look deep inside. The Great One will come," he said.

For several weeks, I prayed and I cried. I changed my diet, stopped smoking cigarettes, took long walks, rested, ate herbs and vitamins, and became weaker and weaker.

One day, Leonard and I met just down the road from his house and I cried, "Leonard, I need a healing."

He replied, "Your healing is within you. Ask the Great One for the power to heal yourself. Go now and heal what needs to be healed the most." He said that as though he already knew what it was.

I left for my spot on the river, a place of quiet and healing, to be in that place, my heart.

I began to chant. I chanted for several hours; then finally, the Great One appeared to me, like never before, but in a way that I always knew was possible. Together with the Great One, Leonard's blessed presence, and my deep faith, conviction, and desire, he came.

"Jay, you have spoken and written on forgiveness, several times, yes?" the Great One asked.

"Yes, I have," I replied.

"Now it's your time. You must forgive yourself for all the misdeeds you have committed in this life and in all lives. This is your time, your opportunity, here in this place finally to forgive yourself. Admit to yourself that you made mistakes, you made errors, and you need to change and grow. Forgive yourself and move on."

I cried like I haven't for a hundred years and said, "Oh, Great One, I cannot. I need your forgiveness. I need to know you love me and forgive me."

Great One replied, *"Now, dealmaker Jay, if I forgive you, will you forgive yourself?"*

I said, "Yes!" and I cried, "You first!"

Great One said, *"I forgive you, I love you,"* and I wept again.

Great One instructed me to release the anger against myself, release fear, let go, and forgive myself for all my wrongdoings, in all lifetimes, in all places, in all events, throughout all of my six billion year history.

"Forgive yourself for all your misdeeds against humanity," Spirit said. *"Forgive yourself for all your misdeeds against all life and all the universes."* Spirit asked that I go deep and look thoroughly and completely for all actions that I considered harmful and went against what I thought of as good conduct, good for self, for spouse, friends, family, plants, animals, Mother Earth, and blessed spiritual beings everywhere in all lifetimes, all space, and all of time. *"Ask for forgiveness, and forgive yourself"* the Great One instructed me to continue. And I did. It took several hours to do so.

Together we, Spirit and I, went into my body for the dis--ease. We found times of hate, anger, deep fear, regret, and very much sadness in several places in and around my body. Together, we removed them, in what is referred to as psychic surgery, only with the Great One's power, there was no blood, no or little pain to endure, and the outcome was nothing less than miraculous.

I found after centuries of shame and blame I could forgive myself. I found love for myself and the Great Spirit that I had never known before and have always craved. I found a connection to spirit that I have never known before that day. The Great One delivered power beyond what I am able to communicate here. He taught me thanksgiving and the importance of gratitude. He taught me the power of being here now and to be thankful for it. He showed me how to heal with this power.

Most importantly, he taught me there is no greater power than love. He asked me to spread my wings, experience peace, love, joy, and healing and asked me to share it and give it freely wherever I went. The Great Spirit asked me to reside in him and to never fear separation again. He told me that we are all one in Him and to see Him everywhere, in everything, and in every person I came into contact with.

"Rise up and sing. All is new. Walk in your new life and know that I love you and I am always with you. Give thanksgiving. Now, rise up and walk new in your renewed, healed, whole body.

"Be kind, be gentle and trust in the love that I give you; you have come to know me. You are healed and—I am."

After several hours of communing with spirit, I came out hungry and exhausted. There was Leonard. "Hi Jay, have you forgiven yourself today?" he asked.

I could barely speak. Leonard said, "You look as though you have been healed today. Fine day for a healing is it not," Leonard asked. "Let's go have a bite to eat and a good drum and talk about it." After a new test from the doctor, all my results were normal.

"Leonard," I said, "I don't want to become a drummer for religion or preach to anyone on the subject of God or tell others how to live their lives."

He said, "That's a good thing. You can, if you wish, just share your story, and those with ears to listen will hear, and those with eyes to see will see, and we love them all just the same whether they hear your story or not. Tell it or not, it's up to you, Jay."

AHO, here is my story.

Great Spirit, come to us in this place,
Come to us that we may know you
And know of your great love and power.
Teach how us to love ourselves and our neighbors
completely
And fully.
Give us your strength each day and lead us into goodness.
Let all men and women know
Of the great peace and joy that we may share
In Love
Through pure love and understanding
In you
In that, there is great healing

Aho

Fall at Bear Claw Mountain

Chapter 15
A Change Has Got to Come

Leonard and I were just hanging out on his ranch one day. The view from Leonard's place looking up to the Lewis and Clark mountain range is breathtaking, especially during the spring wildflower bloom, and the turning of fall, as it was on this day.

Leonard usually looked serene and happy, but not on this day. "Leonard," I said, "you look sad today. What's wrong?"

"My boy, occasionally I become dismayed. My faith gets worn. I must admit it makes me sad." He began to cry deeply.

"A change has got to come," Leonard said. My patience is wearing thin. When will people wake up?" he asked.

"People everywhere are hurting one another. They seem to be unconscious and they are lying, cheating, stealing, hoarding, killing and raping each other, the land and the less fortunate peoples everywhere. Why does this continue to go on?" Leonard asked.

"I am no Pollyanna," he cried, "I know things are hard in the world and it's a rough road. Even young children seem to have little or no respect for the older ones or their own teachers. I know a woman teacher who asked one of her students not to skateboard through the common areas, and out of hate, the student beat her with his skateboard.

"I know this is only one example, but this is what I see as the problem. Not even good manners are applied today. Where does so much anger come from?" he asked. "What makes people want to be so violent? I thought things were changing, but I see they are not.

"Why do people continue to beat one another? Why do needless wars continue?" asked Leonard.

"Once long ago, I was the student of the shaman of our tribe and he taught us to have deep respect for our elders and to follow our roots very closely. What has happened?" he asked. "My prayers have not been answered yet. People have no trust in their hearts, and I cannot see why it is taking so long for them to wake up. I feel like I have failed," said Leonard.

"What is so hard for me to experience," Leonard continued, "is that people know! Deep in their heart of hearts, people know the difference between right and wrong, good and bad, love and evil. But it goes much further into a deep understanding of ethics and morals. It is the cutting edge of kindness, gentleness, and doing good for our neighbor and our fellow man or woman. The cutting edge of goodness—that is the deciding factor in mankind's survival on planet earth.

"I have seen many great leaders in my life," said Leonard. "Along my journey, I have come to know great philosophers, statesmen, poets, writers, shamans, religious leaders, and many of your New Age spokespersons and healers. They have all recognized and spoken of love's power and taught that clean hands make a clean heart. Yet why does stubbornness persist? I see people erring in consistent and huge numbers. I see world hunger; I see the air going so bad it chokes off the oxygen of children at play."

"Leonard, what is the solution to the problem?" I asked. "What is it you want people to see or do?"

Leonard replied, "Love one another! Your books and teachers have covered these subjects very well. I want to see the lessons sink in. When people are able to operate from a place of heart, love, compassion, sharing, and caring beyond what they think they are capable of, they will prosper more than they ever hoped or thought possible. Just look at the last statement of your Jesus Christ dying on the cross, 'Forgive them father, for they know not what they do.' Jesus was trying to get us to love not only our neighbors, but also our enemies. What is so hard for people to understand about this?" Leonard asked.

"How can people do that, Leonard?" I asked.

"By looking deeply and accepting the guidance of the Great Spirit. He will never lead people astray. People know what it means to do onto your neighbor as you would have your neighbor do onto you. People, even unconsciously, know the difference between peace and war, love and hate, friend or foe. No one in a human body on this planet today can say they do not understand these things except out of greed, fear, anger, untruth, mis-guided hate, and just plain stupidity. I have asked you several times in our walks to look, look closely into nature—she holds all of the answers. The love you feel for nature and the nature of man is the love this place needs so very badly. Especially right now."

"Why now? Why does this bother you so, Leonard?" I asked. "Can you just let it go the way it is going? A perfect world is not possible."

"Don't you believe it," Leonard said. "If I have taught you anything, my boy, it is to have faith and believe in all possibilities and in the natural goodness in man and woman, and that anything can happen—goodness is abundant," he said.

"It starts in our imaginations and manifests through our dreams, thoughts, and actions. All life is possible, and all things are possible, with the love of the Great Spirit, the love that is in each of us. That's how we got to these modern times, by dreaming big dreams, dreams that most thought were insane or not possible.

Dreams of great love. Is Shangri-La possible?" Leonard asked.

"Yes, it is," he replied before I could answer.

"What worries me and saddens me," Leonard said, "is that I thought things had changed enough for more people to get this than have. A change has got to come, my boy. There is no other way, before we run out of time."

"Does this have to do with nuclear?" I asked.

"Yes, that, and more," Leonard replied. "It has to with water, air, with fossil fuel consumption, man-made diseases, greed by big-time world control powers, war, hate, fear, jealously, envy, rage, separation, and just plain stupidity. I was hoping to see major changes before I leave this place," he said.

Leonard bounded up with sudden joy.

"Jay, here is a test for you. It is nothing new or original, just a test. Let's see if we can make it work together: you and me, and everyone you know. Go now and find three people who need something, who require assistance in some way. It doesn't matter what it is, how big or how small, rise up and lend a hand. Give, share, put yourself out, go off your normal path, and do something out of the ordinary for someone you know— or someone you do not know—even better that way," said Leonard. "Ask them to recognize what you have done and do not ask nor take anything in return. But do ask them to do the same for three others. Go now. Help three and ask them to help three. Can you just imagine?" Leonard asked, and he cried with excitement.

"While you're at it, write your congress people and senators and ask them to do the same, only on a worldwide basis. Ask them to rid the books of useless out-of-date laws, such as the Ghost Dance being against the law, and to operate from a place of love and ethics. 'Whose ethics?' you may be asking. Their own ethics based on good. Good for the most people everywhere. Good for the environment, the planet, animals, plants, the water, and the rocks. They will look and they will know the creation you are intending by looking into their own hearts. If they do not, elect new ones who will," Leonard said.

"Go now, my boy, save the planet from blowing away. Look at all the things you can do for someone today, every man, every woman, every child. Just start with three and ask them to do the same.

"Here's one more challenge. Before you go, find a way to create world peace and save the environment and planet Earth from destruction. No, too heavy?" Leonard asked. "Okay, just go and do good works for three."

"A change is going come," said Leonard, "when we come from the highest place of the Great Spirit, love, ethics, morals, and deliberate compassion. There is no other way. Let's see if we can wake some more folks up before we run out of time. Even the Dalai Lama said, 'This is the place for people to become free.' Call it, 'Share to Three.'"

"Love one another." It sounds so simple. But it's like Freedom of Speech in the sense that we want to do it when it is our way—but when it has to do with another's thoughts or words or actions, we start back-pedaling, and fast.

What does it mean to love one another? What is love? Love is unconditional. It has to be—or it is just liking a lot for a period of time. Unconditional love loves you when you are otherwise unlovable. Can I love you if you believe differently than I do? Can I love you if you hurt me or someone I love? Can you love me when I am wrong? Can we help one another?

Love for one another, as The Great Spirit put it, love whether we like another person or not. We can dislike someone, their actions, or their ideas, but we are still charged to love them. Loving them is being willing to accept that they are just as entitled as we are to think, believe, speak and act and know right from wrong. "This is in their hearts," Leonard said. "Loving them is wishing the best for them, doing for them, even if they do not feel this way about us. Most of all, love is acceptance," and this is what Leonard longed for.

What a world! Acceptance, love for one another, apart from looking, acting, or thinking alike. Apart from what differences we have. No, we never have to like what we believe is wrong, but we will come a long way when we learn to love people despite our differences and go out of our way to show it.

Let's go out and share this love with three we meet today.

The Ladies at the Dance — 1997 Pow-wow,
Browning MT

Chapter 16
The Pipe Ceremony

One day Leonard said to me, "Occasionally we require a healing; occasionally we require guidance from the Great Spirit. Let's smoke a while, my boy."

Grandfather, hear our words here today. With all of our ancestors and all of our relations, we pray.

Leonard and I walked north, out into the field not far from his house. It was a crystal-clear morning and the view of the Lewis and Clark mountain range was spectacular, with wild flowers in bloom and big, puffy, white clouds overhead. Leonard laid down a Hudson Bay trade blanket and a pipe bundle wrapped in buffalo hide decorated with eagle feathers, and we sat.

"When we smoke the sacred pipe, we ask the spirit of our elders and the Great One to be present with us as we begin," Leonard explained. "The pipe bundle, the pipe, and the tobacco are in themselves sacred and healing, and we ask that our prayers be heard."

Leonard spoke about how smoking the pipe was a tradition in our religion and culture. For centuries The People of the Nation have used the pipe in ceremony and counsel. He told me that long ago a beautiful young woman gifted a beautifully adorned pipe, also wrapped in buffalo hide, to The People. Afterward, she herself became the buffalo and disappeared, but not before she spoke these words:

Friend's Ranch, Way over West, Near Idaho

"Before smoking the pipe, lift it up to the Creator and ask, first to retrieve your soul in the Creator's vision. Ask then for whatever gift you wish to receive or give away.

Point the pipe to the West and give thanksgiving that all darkness has been removed from yourself, The People and the Earth.

Point the pipe to the North and give thanks for purification and for providing all things in all forms.

Point the pipe to the East and ask the Creator for guidance in all ways, things and matters of the heart.

Point the pipe to the South and give praise and thanksgiving for all things in nature and the power to protect and serve her.

After pointing the pipe to the sky and to the earth, fill the bowl with sacred tobacco, clear your mind and inhale the smoke. This is my gift to you from the Creator himself."

Before he began to smoke, Leonard chanted and sang songs in praise and thanksgiving. He lifted the pipe to the West, then to the North, East, and South, and in each direction he gave thanks for our being together that day. He prayed that one day all people would come together in peace and understanding and live as one tribe. "There is no other way," he said.

Leonard handed me the sacred pipe and asked me to smoke and inhale. "This is our sacred pipe. Take it, look at each grain of tobacco, and hold in it in your hand as you would a small child. Cherish this moment, clear your mind, and smoke," he said.

As I sat there with Leonard on this beautiful day, I looked up at the mountain view and the sky above, and just then a bald eagle, sacred to the tribe, flew overhead. Leonard cried, "Fly high; use wisdom!"

I lifted the pipe to smoke and inhale, and as I did I asked the Creator to hear our words of thanks and praise. I prayed that we would be delivered from what no longer served us well. "I ask in your name that the path we are to walk serve only real need, and to let go of the ties that bind our hands and the weight that holds us down," I prayed.

I lifted the pipe to the West and asked that the darkness be lifted and our path only be illuminated.

I lifted the pipe to the North and asked for purification.

I lifted the pipe to the East and asked that the sun bring new life.

I lifted the pipe to the South and asked for guidance from the animal kingdom, that I might be guided on my way.

The bald eagle carried my prayers to the Creator so they could be heard and seen closely by the Great One.

I went into a trance. I got up and danced and I cried in praise to the Creator and to Leonard, my father on the Earth. I gave thanksgiving for the day. This I did for almost an hour, until the heat and exertion brought me back down to my feet and firmly planted me on planet Earth.

"Smoking the pipe today has given you great insight to walk your path," Leonard said. "You have had the great vision so many require. Go out and communicate it to the world, share what you have seen and know, accept gifts, but also give freely. Know that the solution to every problem lies in your own heart, and never disparage your strength to solve these riddles. Try not to get angry at those who do not see, or cannot understand; it is not their time to know of such great power.

"You, my boy, have come to realize your own strength and power. Never give it up. When uncertainty arises, clear your mind, smoke the pipe, and ask for what you wish to see more clearly. The answers have always been with you; they were given to you by the Creator at birth.

"When you share these stories and the way of The People, do not expect any followers. If people do not hear your words, go on your own way, for you have found the path to be of loving service to them, as I am with you here today. With those that do hear, give praise and thanksgiving and allow them to continue on their own way."

Leonard's hope and prayer was always the same, that one day people would be able to look outside of themselves, see the world around them, and find a way to listen and be of service. He always had great hope that this could happen. "People will come together and smoke the pipe", they will find away to love—that was always Leonard's hope.

Leonard and I would smoke the sacred pipe many more times, and each time I could feel myself becoming more aware of the Great Spirit and feel Him in my presence and see my path illuminated. To the Blackfeet people, there is nothing more important than a man knowing his purpose and the way to follow it. I give thanks and praise to the Creator and to Leonard J. Mountain Chief for walking with me every step of my road, even today.

Sometimes, a ceremony must be repeated many times to be effective. Do not give up hope if you try something new once and see little or no difference. Leonard taught the gift of patience, of doing the right thing consistently over time. The path of humankind is not one of instant gratification, as we would like, but one of practicing traditions of reflection, self-evaluation, and communion with nature, and with one another daily, weekly, monthly, yearly, over a lifetime. "It is a process," said Leonard.

Just as a dieter will regain weight after they come off the diet and resume their old eating habits, the seeker of real change must be willing to make real *lifestyle* change. "It is easy to be enthusiastic for a short period of time to achieve a goal, but the true test of your commitment will be a change of the heart," said Leonard. "Change your thinking, and you will change your life. Change your speech and behavior and you will achieve results. Change your story and your life will change. When you achieve results, you are on your way to a meaningful life," said Leonard, "a life of service."

Leonard gifted me a beautifully carved pipe one day and asked that I carry it with me on my way and to take it into ceremony with those who wanted to come in to quiet their mind and retrieve their soul, if even only for a short while. "Look deeply," he said, "and tell them to look deeply also. May their souls be retrieved, renewed, and freed. May they find the true way, the only path that they must walk, in the unfoldment of their soul. There is no other way."

"Leonard," I asked, "Can women participate?"

"Yes," he replied. "Our great women have always practiced the way; they do so in ceremony separate from the men. Their power is so great we do not do ceremony together," he said.

"But remember, Jay, your job is not to teach," He said, "but to guide and listen. Never take the pipe for granted. Smoke only with deep reverence for the Great One and never lead one into ceremony who does not belong there."

Thank you Grandfather.

This Little Badger could dance

Chapter 17
Little Badger's Message

One summer afternoon after a strenuous day's work in my home over on the west side of the mountains in Kalispell, I was sitting at my desk, wondering whether all this work was necessary and worthwhile.

Pammy and I had created an organization called The Birdhouse/Project Bluebird, a business we developed to help bring back the declining Western Blue Bird population. We made painted birdhouses and bird feeders from recycled materials, as well as other artsy objects, which were sold to help raise money for our projects and programs.

We had a staff of seven people, and Leonard was always on the advisory committee. I knew in my heart that the work was of value and that we had a lot going in the way of marketing and fund raising activities. But, as with any business, we had to keep money flowing in to pay the staff and keep the organization running. This became arduous and stressful for me from time to time, and Leonard was always on hand to remind me that the money would come from wherever it was at the time!

Unfortunately, part of my personality was to stress first and figure it out later. So, on one of my most challenging days of trying to figure out how to pay the staff, order materials, and ship off the orders we had, I called Leonard for help. "I'm drowning!" I cried.

"You better come over for a visit," he said. "Come right away!"

Out of respect for Leonard and his commanding way, I said to my wife, "It's Friday; I'm going to see Leonard for the weekend."

She asked if I needed help getting things together for the drive over to Heart Butte.

"Just my fly fishing gear and some coffee," I said. "I think I will make this a mini-vacation at the same time."

The drive east is always fun. It's a beautiful drive along the south edge of Glacier National Park, and the views are relaxing and peaceful. There is always plenty of wildlife to spot, and a nice little coffee shop midway to stop for a stretch and gaze up at the rocky peaks, just outside of Glacier National Park. The air is so fresh it is indescribable. I always compare it to the fragrance of a rose. You can't describe the way a rose smells; you just say it smells great. I was starting to feel a little better even before I arrived at Leonard's.

"It's interesting what a little break and a little detachment can do for one's mind," I thought to myself. I arrived at Leonard's late in the afternoon. His house is not far from the town center of Old Agency, the name given to Heart Butte after U.S. soldiers had settled the area. I drove up close to the house, and there was Leonard with that big smile on his face. He always smiled. He once said it's the best we have to give, a smile, that is.

"Come in, my boy, what are you in the mood for?" asked Leonard. "Bring any coffee?"

"Geez, Leonard, how could I forget coffee?" I asked.

Leonard scooped some soup from the pot on the stove and asked me to sit and take off my boots. "I'll put up the coffee," he said.

"You know, Jay," Leonard said, as if he knew what was on my mind before I could speak and tell him, "People deserve to be happy and joyful. We are completely worthy of peace and need only love in our hearts. Tell me why you are bothered so. Everything always works out; everything is fine, it really is. There is nothing to worry about. Everything is perfect all of the time, even when you don't think it is. This is a hard lesson, even for our people today," he said. "Let us look at what is troubling you. Is it the management, the headaches, the money—or lack of it? Look deeply and tell me exactly, what do you see?"

I looked, and I told Leonard everything that was on my mind. He asked me what color my concerns were, how much they weighed, what they smelled like, what they felt like, and exactly what in the scenario bothered me. I knew he wanted me to look thoroughly and completely.

Leonard said, "You need to look at this as the Little Badger would."

I asked, "How is that, Leonard? Little Badger is the shaman symbol, isn't he?" I asked.

"Yes, of course he is," Leonard said. "The Little Badger is the Shaman, the healer, and that is what he will do today—heal. The Little Badger is also a great hunter and has always out-hunted the coyote. He has the ability to turn every situation from bad to good. Even when hunting is hard, he finds a way to pivot his own energy and make it light and fun. That is just what you need to do today.

"From wherever in your body you hold your challenges, transfer them to your hand. Hold them in your hand and look at them thoroughly and completely, and ask the energy of the scene to turn, to pivot. You must then allow the pivoting to take place. As you are doing this, you might be reminded of some terrible event of long ago, but that does not matter now. You are here now," Leonard said.

"Everything can be easily turned (all energy pivoted)," he said, "by simply looking deeply and using our own strength and power to turn it, to change it, just as the Little Badger would. Turn something bad into something good."

He said, "You folks (referring to people who struggle) are funny. You attach so much importance to every circumstance and think everything is the end of the world. Sure, it is important while you are in your dilemma, but nothing, I mean nothing, is life or death, and everything will always be fine, there is no other way," said Leonard.

"Take your situations, your challenges and what you consider to be your very important problems into your own hands and turn those situations into good outcomes. Don't try to manipulate the outcome," he said, "just allow it to take place. Know in your heart that you are good, that you are deserving and worthy of well-being, perfect harmony, joy, happiness, and love, and abundance. Smile, always smile. Let nothing steal your joy; it's all you have. And be sure to get out of your head from time to time.

"Little Badger was a great hunter," Leonard said, "and so are you. Go beyond mere survival and achieve everything you set out to. It is your given right to be happy, and prosperous. The Creator wants nothing less for you. All you have to do is recognize this and allow yourself to experience the happiness, love, and joy you seek, and be thankful for it. Your organization is already a huge success. Now just allow it to be—and smile." He laughed and told me to go down to the Two Medicine River and catch some trout for our breakfast the next morning.

"If you meet Little Badger on the way," he said, "feed him a trout and give praise and thanksgiving to him for the lesson of complete and total allowance and the ability to experience joy."

The following Monday back at the office, a huge cash order came in and everything was fine; it really was. I am grateful that Leonard taught me the best medicine, to take life reverently, but not too seriously, and to accept myself as well as others. He taught me to laugh and to laugh at myself. Most of all, he taught me to live and allow.

Charlie Mountain Chief, My Brother, in Full Traditional Eagle Regalia

Jay, Leonard, Dee, Katrina, Rose, and Their Children

Chapter 18
Leonard's Message to the People on Family

There was to be a gathering, a pow-wow of sorts, at the round lodge in Heart Butte. It was a time for dance and speeches from the elders of the Blackfeet Nations, and the only non-Natives to attend were married into the tribe or adopted. Leonard was to be one of the key speakers, and his subject on this day was family.

Pammy and I were invited to set up a booth for Project Bluebird at the event and to give a small presentation on our goals and projects for the organization. We knew about the event several weeks before it would occur, so we had plenty of time to create our booth. We were extremely honored to be invited, and our intention was to make Leonard proud to have us there.

Pammy, as everyone used to call her, was also deeply in love with Leonard and had huge respect for him. She was very happy about my connection with him and always allowed me the time and space to be with him whenever he called for a one-on-one visit. She never felt left out, nor complained that I spent so much time with him.

One day in 1993, Pammy said, "Someday you will write about your time with Leonard and people will come to know him and love him just as you do, Jay." She was right.

Now, one thing I think I might as well point out is that everything on the Res is done in Native time, which means nothing gets started on time, at least not according to White man's concept of "on time." Pammy and I were very eager to get our booth set up, so when folks started to arrive, they could come over for a visit and a short presentation to help them understand what we were up to. We packed our truck the night before and left the house at four a.m. so we could get to the lodge by six and set up. Thing was, nobody else got there till around ten a.m. Some didn't arrive till noon. The event was scheduled to start at nine a.m., but it didn't really get going until around four or five that afternoon.

People wandered in around two p.m. and three p.m., and they were talking and eating the food that was put out, including my favorite, Indian fry bread. After a while, the drum songs started, and many of The People pulled chairs around in a circle to watch the dancing that started to take place. Leonard came over to me and asked that I join him in the circle and dance a while. I cried I was so happy to be asked, and joined in the dance, which went on for several hours. Leonard remarked, "Gets you high, doesn't it? Who needs drugs? This is all one needs to get high and out of the body."

I laughed and replied, "Yes, Leonard. We do not need drugs. Our tribe is not a peyote tribe; it does not grow naturally in the area, and we never use any substance for our visions."

The drumming and dancing went on for hours. We did not stop for water or food; we just danced, meditated, and prayed. After the dance was over, there was a short give-away, where grandmothers expecting new babies from their daughters gave away gifts in prayer for the child's good health and long life. There were gifts for the ill, the poor, and people in need on the Res.

Then the Chief of the tribe (Earl Goodhearted) stood up and said, "It is time for us to speak." The elders stood up one at a time to name their subject and to speak on it. Some spoke about tribal politics, some about the water, others about the harvesting of timber, and so on. There were tribal leaders from all four separate regions of the tribe, two from Montana and two from Canada, where many of The People had fled during the last war with the Whites in 1894. When the wars came to an end, The People settled.

Then Leonard rose to his feet to speak.

"My brothers and sisters, we are a family," he shouted. "It is family that ties us, and nothing is more important than this. We are one family and whatever disagreements we have ever had must end today, as we recognize that we are one family with our white brothers and sisters and with dark-skinned people of all Nations." Leonard asked that we quiet our minds and allow this family into our experience. The People looked upon him with wonder, some with enthusiasm in anticipation of what he was about to say.

"Quiet now," he said, "quiet your mind. Breathe deeply. Relax and breathe, close your eyes, breathe. We are one family. Breathe and allow your mind to become quiet, whatever noise you hear, whatever pictures appear, and allow them to simply pass through you and on their way. Breathe, relax your brain, relax your head, and relax your facial muscles. Let the tension in your neck and shoulders melt away. Relax and breathe. Relax your entire body; breathe into your chest and abdomen. Relax. Let your hands fall to your sides. Just drift and breathe. Relax your ankles and toes, and breathe.

"Now, notice a small purple dot right in the middle of your forehead between your eyes. Feel this dot as warm, loving and comforting. Breathe and be with this purple dot," said Leonard.

"Breathe. Now expand the purple dot all over your face and head and allow it to radiate down your chest and back and cover your body, back and front, tip to toe. Feel the warmth and love of this dot all over your body, and breathe. Do not worry if it becomes arousing. Allow yourself to experience the joy. Now push the purple dot outward to include the energy around your body, and then out to your neighbors sitting right next to you.

"Allow your family to feel the compassion and love and happiness created by the purple dot. Let the purple dot fill the room and have every person in the room feel the gift of the purple dot.

"Now push the purple dot out to cover the entire tribal Nation and allow all of our people to notice its radiance. Continue to breathe. Relax and push the purple dot out over the Nation of the Americas and allow all tribes, all people, to feel the warmth and peace.

"Expand your dot to include all people everywhere and allow them to be your loving family. Allow your love for one family to be felt by all people and all creatures. Allow the tobacco plant to feel your loving, healing energy and ask in prayer that all do the same.

"Breathe; relax. Breathe love, breath peace, breathe love, breathe joy, and breathe love for one family everywhere. Allow the purple dot to become one purple dot, shared in harmony, love, compassion, and joy by all beings everywhere in all universes, and let it be. Be silent and breathe.

After a few minutes; Leonard said, "And now, as you come back into this room, in this time and place, and begin to open your eyes, know that there is no war, there is no separation. Know we are one family. From this day on, we exclude no one from the way," said Leonard.

In the year 1994, the four Nations of the Blackfeet that had been separate for nearly one hundred years came together in peace and to re-form as one Nation.

Two are Always Better than One on the Res

149

White Buffalo Calf Woman, the Lakota Matriarch

Chapter 19
Morning Star

Morning Star, a beautiful Maiden of Blackfeet legend, is one of the most important Matriarchs of the Blackfeet tribe's oral history, and on this night it was no different.

Leonard and his wife, Dee, came over west to Kalispell for a visit and to take care of some business in the town nearby. Leonard had called the night before to let us know he and Dee would be in town and would stop by to see us. The one thing Leonard liked as much as my coffee was Pammy's baking, and I informed him there would be a fresh huckleberry pie waiting for them when they arrived. He said he would be on time for dinner and laughed.

Pammy and I were excited over the thought of their visit, and we eagerly awaited their arrival. We cleaned the house. I fried up mom's fried chicken and in between baking, Pammy washed the windows. She even told me to take out the trash, my least favorite job around the house. I'll wash dishes, do the laundry, and even clean the bathroom bowl, but please don't make me take out the trash—okay so I did it.

"Oh, my God, it's only four o'clock in the afternoon. Who's that driving up the road?" I asked.

Pammy said, "Very funny, go out there and greet them." I don't know what she was so nervous about; it was only Leonard and Dee, but Pammy had such deep respect for Leonard that she felt a little intimidated by him. He was huge in stature, handsome beyond compare, and I think his power, knowingness and ability to really look at a person was somewhat startling to my wife.

"Hey, Leonard, how's it going? What are you doing here so early?" I asked, as I kissed Dee on the cheek and invited them in.

On the way to the house, Leonard remarked that he was getting to know himself better all the time and that the drive was getting to be too long for him. He apologized for making me do it so often.

"Are you kidding?" I replied. "Come in, my home is yours for as long as you want to stay."

"Got any coffee?" Leonard asked.

"Geez Leonard," I said, "just come in."

We sat in the living room for awhile. Leonard loved to come to my house because I used to be in the art business and still had quite a collection around the house. He liked to talk about art of the West and the old days of which it reminded him. Leonard told us that his father knew Charles M. Russell, a famous Montana artist from the late 1800's, a great friend of the Blackfeet tribe.

The West that Leonard knew wasn't the Old West of the movies or 1950's TV. Leonard spoke of the West in which being in nature was a way of life. He recalled the West of hard work, not government aid, and told us of the West that didn't have to be "won," but was shared freely with all who worked her, respected her, and called her home.

Pammy and I owned a rather large six bedroom home on forty acres with a barn and other out buildings, and Leonard loved to roam around and look at everything. I've loved Native American and Western art all of my life and fell into buying and selling it as a way to supplement my collecting. I never thought much of it, but Leonard thought it was kind of neat to know an art dealer.

We visited for a few hours and we had our meal along with the freshly baked huckleberry pie, just out of the oven, and plenty of coffee. We made our way back into the living room to sit by the fire, and Leonard asked if we knew of Morning Star. I replied that I had only heard the name. Leonard looked over his shoulder at Dee, smiled and said, "She is sacred to us and a very important Indian leader to many tribes," and they smiled at each other again.

"The maiden Morning Star came to teach the meaning of life to The People of the Nations," he explained. "She came to show us the way to our true purpose for being here."

"And what is that?" I asked.

"Love, my boy, and the true unfoldment of spirit." Leonard took a deep breath and relaxed himself into a more comfortable position. "Unfoldment is the way we come to know exactly who we are, and there is no higher purpose than to love another," he said.

"Many learned men speak of these things in riddles and poems," Leonard continued. "The clergy preach on the subject, and teachers in schools help students to examine the way of unfoldment, but it is to no avail if there is no love. We cannot simply examine this thing; we must experience it in order to fulfill our destiny."

Leonard closed his eyes and continued telling us about Morning Star. "Morning Star came to a young couple on the prairie one day while the two were romancing. They wanted very much to share the love and joy they felt for one another, but they were from two separate tribes. Their unfoldment was frowned upon by their people, and they were discouraged from seeing one another. Morning Star startled the young couple with her sudden appearance, and the young woman recognized her before the young man did. She asked, 'You are of the Great Spirit, are you not?'

Morning Star replied that this was so, and she began to speak, "*It is time that you come to know yourselves and to know that spirit always looks after you. It is time for you to know that laws set up by Man are not always useful and that you must follow your own way. Look deeply into your hearts, see who you really are, and guide your life according to your own rules. Do not depend on others' laws, which are outside your own faith, belief, and trust. Look into one another's eyes; look into one another's hearts, and see. Use your gift of intuition, use your knowingness, and forget about books and other's teachings. Look deeply and you may come to recognize there is no higher purpose than the unfoldment of the soul in love.*

You are here for a very short while. What seems like years is only a moment in time, and you have this opportunity to feel and express deep love. Do not waste this chance; it may not come again, for many are like the Goose Tribe. They mate only once, and it is a lifetime of love and when separated, it will not come again. In this, your unfoldment lies. Love like there is no tomorrow because tomorrow may never come. There is only now, unfolding in love.

Some may never come to know this path of unfoldment. Only the very fortunate see this gift presented to them. Turn away from it and you refuse life."

Morning Star reminded the young couple of the importance of honesty and communication. "Love deeply," she said and disappeared.

The young couple looked into each other's eyes and said, "I choose unfoldment. I choose love. I love you."

Leonard opened his eyes and said, "We are very fortunate to have Morning Star to guide us. We all smiled and felt relaxed and poised in love.

154

Ah Uh Op Vista Doggie
Vista Doggie Ah He
God Bless you, God Bless us all.

Artist – Cochrane

Chapter 20
Friendship

A friend of mine in Kalispell, MT once asked, "You spend so much time with Leonard. Is he a friend as well as a mentor and teacher? Do you and he ever do anything together just for fun?"

"Well, yes, a lot," I replied. "Leonard is one of the most jovial men I have ever known. He loves to laugh, he tells pretty good jokes, and he has a wonderful trickster coyote personality." The truth is Leonard was my friend and my buddy and my teacher all at the same time.

It was March and Great Falls, Montana was celebrating Charlie Russell Week. This is a full week devoted to Western art shows, with exhibits, auctions, and sales set up at every hotel in town. Most old traders arrive a few days early, and many stay for days after the official shows are over. Leonard called to ask if I would be going.

"Are you kidding?" I replied, "This is my week of the year, my opportunity for good income and to see art dealers from all over the world. Besides, the parties are the best."

"Can I come along?" he asked.

"Why sure, Leonard, I would love to have you come with me," I said.

After packing up all my trade gear, paintings, Native collectables, antique firearms, personal gear, and a few museum-quality beaded pieces, I kissed Pammy so-long, and headed east of the mountains to pick up my traveling partner, Leonard.

On my way out the door, Pammy said, "You two be good now!" Pammy liked to come along sometimes too, but with six horses, six dogs, seven cats, and topical fish, not to mention the indoor plants and the Birdhouse business, somebody had to stay at home.

The drive down to Great Falls from Heart Butte is about two and half hours, and Leonard, at nearly seventy years old, was like an excited, little boy. He couldn't wait to get there. He had heard about this event for years but never had the opportunity to attend, and he wouldn't stop with all the questions and the stories he had heard about the event and the parties. Some of the tales were true, but most were only built-up rumors of wild women and such.

When we got to the hotel I was booked at for the show, I went to check-in, and the place was already buzzing with dealers. Leonard and I walked up to the desk and I paid for the two rooms. Leonard said, "By golly, Jay, why can't we bunk together like we do when we go camping?"

"We *are* going to bunk in the same room, Leonard," I replied. "One room is to set up my show of goods for sale; the other is for "bunking"." That's how it works at Charlie Russell Week. All the dealers need one or two rooms for the show and another to try to get some sleep in.

Jay in His Display Room at the Russell Week,
Great Falls, MT, 1994

This was a neat hotel to set up in because the auction part of the sale takes place on the center floor and the rooms on all levels open to a great view of it. The display rooms stay open as long as the dealers are in the rooms and can stand on their feet, which in most cases means all night long and all day too. Leonard was excited about the notion of staying up all week.

The whole town is taken up by the event: the high school auditorium, the fairgrounds, all of the hotels, coffee shop lobbies, and gas station offices. Everyone has something for sale. Even the weekend yard sales are some of the best and most interesting in the whole country this time of year. Leonard looked like a boy in a candy store.

We had the great opportunity to be invited to one of the most exclusive after-show parties of the entire event, held at the best hotel in town, The Heritage. When we got there, the ballroom was filled with the world's richest dealers, important businessmen, and movie stars. It was the first time I had been invited to that particular party. Leonard brought his fiddle, and he was the hit of the evening.

Leonard was amazed all week by the millions of dollars in value of the art all over town: paintings, bronzes, antique books and documents, Native art, antique firearms, coins, and you name it, all being traded or paid for with briefcases full of cash.

Limousines lined the streets, and movie stars were close at hand for conversation. Leonard had been a part-time actor and had appeared in several small films, but I had never seen him star struck before. He stayed pretty close by most of the week and witnessed sales and purchases in the thousands of dollars, cash money. Leonard was never wealthy money-wise and had never seen so much cash change hands in one place his whole life.

159

One day during the week, we heard about a completely Native show at one of the auditoriums in town and we both wanted to see the show and sale. We made our way across town through a maze of cars and pedestrians and found the spot where the show and sale were taking place.

"This is wonderful." Leonard said. "Look at all this Native work."

We walked the show and met with contemporary artists and dealers of antique Native art. We came across a collection of depictions by a famous Lakota artist named Amos Bad Heart Buffalo. These drawings are the only known Native drawings of the famous Battle of the Little Big Horn River, and they were in museum-quality condition. I bought the collection for $14,000, knowing I would have a good customer for them later. Leonard's eyes bugged out of his head. He remarked that it was a lot of money, and I said, "Yes it is, but that is the art market. From time to time you have to spend a lot of money to make some."

Leonard said he thought people could only have the money they believed they could have and I replied, "Yep, it pretty much works that way, doesn't it?" He went on to give me his thoughts about money: having it, earning it, and spending it. "Money is an interesting thing," he said. "Many only have enough to barely get by, and some have none, while others have more than they can ever use. Nevertheless, it's all the same. It's a tool is it not."

I said, "Yes, I know that, Leonard."

"What is interesting to me," Leonard said, "is the concept of prosperity, wealth, and riches. I have come to realize that people can have as much money as they can have. It's not so much a feeling of worthiness or deserving, as it is the ability to have it, to possess it, save it, spend it, give it away. It's all the same. How much can we have? How much can we have in our lives? It is very much an individual thing, isn't it?"

"Yes, Leonard," I said, "I believe it is."

"Funny," he said, "I never felt poor without a lot of cash."

"Leonard," I replied, "you are among the richest men I know."

We had a load of fun that week. We attended some great parties, met some interesting folks, ate like pigs, got very little sleep and made loads of money. Leonard never had a lot of money, but he was one of the happiest, richest persons I have ever known. Leonard didn't judge a person by the thickness of his wallet, but by his character. He knew that money couldn't buy the most important things. Money couldn't fix the plight of the Native Americans, or reverse the effects of the Holocaust, or bring our loved ones back to this earth when they passed beyond. It was love and friendship that mattered to him most. One thing for sure is Leonard has always been a dear friend of mine, and no amount of money could buy that—not ever.

White Buffalo Speaks on Jay's Vision Quest, Eastern Montana near the Dakota's State Line, 1997

Jay and White Buffalo Speaks

Chapter 21
White Buffalo Speaks

The People of the Nation, like people in cultures throughout the world, especially in Christian, Hindu, and Buddhist countries, hold certain deities in high regard. They value the deities' presence and impact on their lives and even depend on their words for their very survival.

White Buffalo Speaks has never been an embodied entity—he's a spirit who has never walked on the Earth in a body, but he has been an important communicator for The People as long as anyone can recall. In some Native cultures, White Buffalo is known as Calf Woman, a feminine entity. I came to know of White Buffalo Speaks through Agnes, an elder woman of the Blackfeet Nation, who told me this story.

A very long time ago there were two young hunters out on the prairie, hoping to spot buffalo so the tribe could come back and take them for the winter's meat supply. The young men traveled far but did not find buffalo tracks that would lead them to a herd.

They had traveled so far from camp that they had become lost. They sat in confusion and asked one another, "What should we do? We are lost, and we have found no buffalo to hunt, and The People shall surely starve if we are not successful." They began to cry, "Oh Great One, lead us, lead us to the herd and back home again."

Just then there was a lightning burst in the sky that separated the clouds from the heavens and White Buffalo Speaks appeared.

"Why do you whine so? Have you no faith? I am the greatest hunter in the land and I always lead you. Where is your trust? Do you believe for an instant that I would let my people go hungry?" White Buffalo Speaks asked, and he showed the boys the way to the herd and the way home.

Before his departure, White Buffalo Speaks asked the boys to know his name and he gave them a gift.

"Know that I am White Buffalo Speaks, the one who unfolds all mystery and names you as my vessels to talk to The People. Those who hear my words will know who I am; those who do not will never hear me, not even with your voice. Speak through me only when requested."

In 1997 Leonard and I were out driving around the Res after the public pow-wow that summer, and Leonard said to me, "There is someone I want you to meet. Let's go over to where the elders stay." We drove up to a building where lots of old people were sitting around, outside and in.

As we got out of the truck and began to walk towards the building, we saw a very old woman named Agnes. She pointed her finger at me and began to laugh very hard. She spoke broken English, and at first, it was hard for me to understand what she was saying.

"I know why you are here," she said. "You are here to hear the words of White Buffalo Speaks," and she laughed again. "Come sit by Agnes," She said.

Leonard looked at me and smiled. "This is a very good day," he said. "We will dance a very special Friendship Dance when we go home."

Agnes took a deep breath and went into an immediate trance and began to speak in Native tongue, and even though I had never understood the words before, I clearly understood them that day.

She spoke of the days when The People were free to walk and hunt. She spoke of The People today and their politics and challenges. She spoke of the water and how it was unsafe to drink, and she spoke a prophecy about what was to come, although the words she spoke were not her words. They were the words of White Buffalo Speaks who came to guide the way.

"White Buffalo Speaks was gifted to me many years ago," Agnes said, and then White Buffalo spoke these words:

"The way for all peoples must be heard. There is healing and coming into being that needs to be done. People need to be acknowledged, need to be heard and understood, and that is when they will be able to proceed on to their own next level of unfoldment."

I was almost in shock. I could feel shivers all through my body, and I was holding back my tears of joy at the experience.

When Agnes came out of the trance, she said, "I am old now, and my time here is not long. Only those that can hear the words of White Buffalo Speaks will hear them, and I gift him to you this day." She gave me a beautiful piece of jewelry, which symbolized the spirit of White Buffalo Speaks, and asked me to guard it well.

"I give him to you," she said, "take him, know he is always with you, and use his words in your life. Use his words to help heal and to retrieve your soul and the souls of your loved ones, and to bring forth the coming," by which she meant the unfoldment of our spirit into exactly who we are and the way we walk. "He is yours now," she said.

I became weak and dizzy and almost passed out. Agnes grabbed my hand and said, "Yes, his presence is powerful, and you will get used to how to handle his energy in your body. Never speak of him lightly. Speak of him only in deep reverence. He speaks the words of the Great Spirit, and he himself is very powerful. Use his words, follow his lead, and never divulge his words to those that cannot hear." She started to laugh again and said goodbye.

I began to cry. "Why me, Leonard?" I asked. "Why not a person of The Nation?"

"She trusts you," he replied.

We got back into Leonard's old Ford pickup truck, and I could not speak. We drove up to Two Medicine Lake and sat for a while, and Leonard asked me to speak with White Buffalo Speaks.

I closed my eyes took a deep breath and asked for White Buffalo Speaks' presence, and I could feel the same sensation I had felt when Agnes told me he was now the spirit I would communicate with for The People. Leonard asked questions. He wanted to know about the future of The People. He asked about the environment and the challenges all people might face, and the answers flowed out of my mouth, calmly and confidently in reply. After a while, the communication came to a stop, and Leonard smiled and gave me a hug.

The answers to Leonard's questions are in the next few chapters. Use these words or not. Sometimes answers come in forms we expect, sometimes not. When we ask a question, we must be prepared not only for the answer, but for the way in which it comes and what we do with it when it comes. We walk in the lessons we learn or we ignore them. White Buffalo Speaks is with me here today, as is the spirit of Leonard.

Middle Fork of the Flathead River

Sundance: A Time For Celebration, A Time For Coming Into Being,

Chapter 22
Sun Dance

There is a time for coming into manhood, a time for unfoldment, and a time for renewal of the spirit.

It was August, and Pammy and I were over east for a little vacation on the Res. We had come to fish, hike, and relax. We were camped on Twin's Lake, right across the road from Leonard's small, barn-red house and just a stone's throw from fourteen different rivers and two hundred lakes, with pretty easy access to most of them. Even the ones that were less-than-easy to get to were not really a hard hike. Being August, it was hot and beautiful. Fortunately, mosquitoes are not an issue over east because the wind is usually blowing!

Pammy was a beautiful woman with thick blond hair and dark blue eyes, but the most interesting thing I have to share about Pammy is that she was the most giving person I have ever known in my life. I would not have been able to have these wonderful experiences with Leonard and The People if Pammy hadn't been so supportive. She enjoyed much of it with me and allowed me to experience the rest of it on my own. It made her happy for me to be with Leonard.

We had a special relationship of trust and respect and always attempted to encourage each other in their pursuits. This built a trust between us, a sense of security that our experience, whether shared or separate, would enrich us individually as well as our relationship. I will always appreciate Pammy's willingness to share her passions with me, and the way she encouraged me to share mine with her. Love does things in ways we don't even know about at the time.

We had been camped at our site for two weeks and had visited Leonard and his family a few times during our stay. Leonard and his family lived very simply, without a lot of things around the house other than family photos, but his house was always warm and comfortable and we always felt at home walking in.

While visiting Leonard's house, we heard on more than one occasion about the annual Sun Dance that was going to take place soon. It was nearing the end of our vacation and time to go home. On a Thursday afternoon, Pammy and I started to get our things together so we could leave the following morning. Leonard came down from the house to our camp and said he had news for us.

"What's up, Leonard?" I asked. "Geez, this has been a wonderful vacation. We caught plenty of trout and had a good rest, and we're heading out in the morning. I wish we had more time to visit."

"Well, my boy, we may not have time to visit this trip, but you and your wife have been invited to Sun Dance. Would you like to come?" he asked.

Not many non-Natives are invited to Sun Dance. I looked at my Pammy. We smiled and said, "Leonard, it would be our honor."

Sun Dance is a rather intense, private time of drumming, chanting, fasting, and spirit talk for The People. It was to start the following day and go on four days and, as we would find out, there would be no sleeping during this event. Those who are familiar with Sun Dance know that this is the time when young men's bodies are pierced as part of the ritual rite of passage into adulthood. Through hours of dance, chanting, praying, and fasting, the young men go into a trance and feel no pain when they are pierced and tied to a buffalo skull or a tree, and spikes made from dear horn are driven through their skin. They hang there for hours until the ties are broken and the young men break free into manhood.

Pammy and I packed up our old white Ford pickup and moved our camp up the hill on Little Badger Creek onto open land below the Lewis and Clark Mountains with the millions of trees above us.

The Sun Dance was to be held in a small, remote canyon with a spectacular view of the mountains above and the prairies below.

The People of Heart Butte, Browning, and Cut Bank, Montana started to arrive shortly after we got there until there were about four hundred of us. The men got the fire going, the women helped set up a makeshift camp, and everyone seemed to be in good spirits, except for the young men, who were nervous about being pierced in the next few days. Pammy and I participated in whatever we could to help set up teepees and such and were happy and excited to be there.

After a few hours had gone by, the drumming and the singing of Native songs started, and people began to gather in a circle and wish one another well. The women offered gifts in a give-away ceremony. The men started to dance, and this would go on for four days. There is no food for the dancers during this period, and anyone else that wanted to participate in the fast could do so. Women do not Sun Dance and are not pierced.

Small groups of people would move out of the larger group and form into small groups to sing, have conversations, and pray. Leonard asked Pammy and me to join in his small group and he introduced me as the speaker of White Buffalo Speaks.

He asked that I allow White Buffalo Speaks to come and speak with The People, and The People let out an "aw...." They seemed impressed, happy, and excited to hear the words he would speak.

We sat on the ground on a small knoll not far from the main campfire and activities. I took a deep breath and immediately went into trance. The words of White Buffalo Speaks came through me:

"My People, brave ones here today, hear my words and take them to heart. This is your place; this is the place for all men and women to be free. This is the place where you find your true nature, happiness and joy, but this is also the place that needs your love, your help, your support, and activity.

I have spoken with your Mother Earth, and she is not happy. She thinks you are trying to kill her. She says she is choking; the air is not fit to breathe, the water is not fit to drink, and she cannot understand why you are not respectful of her.

You poison her with chemicals used in mining and agriculture, you throw gases up into the air so that no living thing can be well. You test bombs in her oceans and allow the great fishes to wash ashore and die. Mother Earth asks why you do not respect her. She says, "I have given them all they require: clean air, water, good foods for their bodies, and this is their response to me. I fly up into the mountains and see the trash they leave behind. Do they really believe tin cans and broken glass belong there? Why do they have no respect?" she asks.

Mother Earth came to me, White Buffalo Speaks, and she pleaded, "We have such little time left before they kill this place. What is wrong? Have they not eyes nor nose nor brains? Where is their respect? They have developed nuclear bombs, they have developed mustard gas, and they have made bug killers and sprays of all kinds. Is it only gold that interests them? Why don't they have respect? One day this place will not be here, and then where will they dance?"

White Buffalo Speaks went on to say, *"You people have so much understanding, you know so much. You are the co-creators of this environment; you can have anything you want. What is it you want? Clean air? Clear water? An environment that is not deteriorating? Wild creatures that are not heading for extinction? Just imagine and ask yourself what you truly want. When you can imagine it and see it clearly, it is yours. You already know of such things. You know that whatever your heart desires, the Creator supplies, so why would you not want a clean, safe environment, free from harmful chemicals and rays from the sun that can kill your children? When will you feel it is important enough to influence your governments, your heads of state, and your neighbors to look after your Mother? Without her there is nothing else. There is nowhere else to dance. The choice is yours. I leave you with that."*

When I opened my eyes, I saw The People smiling and shaking their heads in agreement. Each member of our circle came over to greet my wife and me, and many presented a gift offering.

Sundance ended with many newly arrived men. The people made new decisions to look after Mother Earth. Leonard said, "Good Sundance, eh!" And he asked, "So, who is the teacher now?"

Leonard said, "We have work to do, don't we?" and I agreed. Leonard passed in 1999, and we still have a long way to go.

White Buffalo Speaks and our Mother do not understand what is holding things up-when will they wake up.

The Medicine Wheel: East of the Blackfeet Nation, over on the Rocky Boy Res -- in place for 14,000 Years

Chapter 23
Ghost Dance

Many Native rituals have been performed for several thousand years, but during the U.S. Indian Wars, some of them, including The Ghost Dance, were outlawed. I can't help but wonder why the U.S army would outlaw a religious event of Native peoples— unless they believed in its power. The Ghost Dance calls in the spirits of those who have been lost to death. It calls back the elders and asks for their counsel, strength, and power, which it is believed gives personal strength and power to the participants in the ceremony. The law against performing the Ghost Dance is still on the books today.

I was attending a public pow-wow in Browning, Montana with Leonard in 1993. During this annual event, the Blackfeet and other tribes come together in a festive way to compete and display for the public their dances and dance outfits. There are food booths, crafts for sale, and Native gambling games. Most public pow-wows go on for two or three days, and often Natives gather nearby to participate in more traditional rituals and ceremonies, which are not open to non-Natives.

Leonard approached me and asked, "Do ghosts scare you, Jay?"

"Only if they go 'Boo!' in the night," I replied, and Leonard let out a hardy burst of a laugh.

"We, The People of the Nations, have been calling back our ancestors for many years," he said. "It's called a Ghost Dance. Would you like to come with me tonight and join in on the ceremony?"

I said, "Yes, Leonard, I would love it."

Leonard's family and I were camped at the pow-wow in Browning where we had our teepees, cook tents, and "what-not" all set up, and we were in no mood to move the camp. We had participated in the day's events, danced the Friendship Dance, watched the competitions, and had returned to camp to have a meal with the family. It was about eleven p.m. and just turning dark when Leonard came over to where I was having a lovely conversation with a Native woman about the Indian ways.

"I hate to interrupt," he said, "but it's time we go."

I looked at him, looked at her, and said, "Okay, let's go."

She smiled and said, "Have good ceremony." I never mentioned to her where we were would be going. She seemed to just know.

Leonard and I arrived up on a piece of property owned by another elder of the tribe, which sits at the foot of some of the most spectacular mountains in Glacier National Park, not far from Kiowa Creek. We had a beautiful view in the full moon that night. There were about a hundred pick-up trucks already parked up on a knoll when we got there, and we could hear the drumming and singing when we got out of Leonard's truck. As we approached the ceremony, I could see it was all men dancing, wearing only enough clothes to cover their privates. The drumming was very intense, and the singing was loud like screaming. Many of the men were deep in trance. Leonard and I immediately took off our clothes and joined the dance.

Almost right away, I started to have visions of family and friends who had passed away not long ago. I could clearly hear their voices join in on the singing.

We danced for several hours. I had a vision of a mass of tribal members dancing all around us, but their bodies were only light forms. Great ones of the past came to dance in the ceremony; icons from every culture, holy men of White and Native culture, came to join in as well. Their names might surprise you but I will not mention them here, except to say that White Buffalo Speaks joined in the dancing, as did several of my family members who were no longer with their bodies.

We danced till dawn, and during one rest Leonard and I sat in counsel and spoke in the Native tongue with our welcomed guests. Leonard began. He said, "Some call you ghosts, some refer to you as entities. It does not matter what label you are given. Jay and I know you to be real, and we hear your voices. We welcome you and we are glad you are here with us this day. We welcome your presence and, we welcome your loving support. We ask those of other than pure intention to leave this place for you are not welcome in counsel. Great Ones, we ask that you speak to us in our times of need. Help show us the way. Give advice when asked and carry us when we are too weak to walk on our own. Lend us your power and strength this day and join in our joyful experience and dance in this place. We give praise and thanksgiving for your being here. Be near always. We ask that you strengthen us, so that your power may be useful and that we will help others. Let us hear your words clearly, and give us the confidence to follow the way."

Then he said, "It is your time to speak, Jay," and I began. I said, "I have felt your presence for many years, and I have known your energy for a very long time. I now see you clearly and invite you to be here whenever you like. I need your love, support and guidance, for I was never meant to walk alone in this life, and I value your friendship. I will from this day forward refer to you as counsel and I recognize your great strength and power, and I give thanks for your presence. Know that you are welcome, and even when I recognize one as less-than-friendly, I will allow you in this space while recognizing your negative intentions. I also ask that you go off and do ritual to find a way to become free of your evil ways. I recognize the great, pure, and good ones present here. I hear your voices clearly, in and out of my dreams. Please help guide my way and the way of The People. I give praise and thanksgiving."

Leonard and I sat quietly for a very long time just looking into one another's eyes and cherishing the moment. "Good night for a Ghost Dance, is it not?" Leonard asked.

"Yes, Leonard," I replied, "a very good night."

Since that time, counsel has never left my side, and I am conscious of their presence daily. I have several photos taken of myself where one can clearly see the image of White Buffalo Speaks by my side.

When Leonard passed in 1999, I played the drum song for him. He came to me on that cool March night and asked that I never feel alone. He is always with me as a member of counsel now and reminds me that there is no death. "It is nothing but a transition," he said. "Never fear it."

Just East of the Blackfeet Res, west of the badlands

Chapter 24
Grass Dance

Every year in September at harvest time, The People come together for a Grass Dance to drum, dance, feast, and celebrate the abundance the Great Spirit has shared with the tribe. On the far east side of the Res, there is a place known as the Sweetgrass Hills, named for a fair maiden who gave her life for unrequited love. Below these buttes lie the great plains of eastern Montana, and The People have gathered here for centuries on this ground, known as the common ground, where we come together in common good, to dance and give thanks to the Creator for all his gifts.

This September was no surprise because it had a little of everything: hot air, warm showers, and heavy wind. Leonard used to tell me, "Don't come over here and cuss this wind, because if you do, it will surely blow the roof right off my house," which is to say the wind blows a lot over east.

The People love the Sweetgrass Hills for the Grass Dance. The grass reminds them of long ago when it was knee high, long before the buffalo were gone and replaced by English cattle. They also appreciate being at the foot of one of the tribe's most sacred mountains. And the view to the west back to the Rockies is unbelievable.

Everyone is welcome at this event, although not many non-Natives show up. It is not a pow-wow, and there is no entertainment to speak of, no booths and no stick games nor gambling. The People are there to give thanks for the gifts of life and to dance to the drum song in the sun.

It is no small gathering; tribal folks from near and far come to attend. There are giveaways for good luck and some pretty good eating. It is a daylong event, and most make a long drive home when it is over. As I would be doing because I was needed back in the office for work on project Bluebird the following day. I made the drive home in three and half hours that night.

The People gathered in large groups to hear the speeches of anyone that wished to speak or pray. These days the tribal leaders bring along a battery power loudspeaker so everyone can clearly hear the speaker, and no one is discouraged from talking.

When it was Leonard's turn to speak, he stood up and said: "O Great Spirit, you bring us many gifts; you give us our beautiful children, our homes, and plenty to eat, and we give thanks. You give us our women and the many gifts they bring to the men. We cherish these great gifts and the gifts to come. We see clearly that what we need, you provide us, and we give thanks. We feel deep in our hearts we are deserving of these blessings, and you continue to shower us with goods, with money, and with the clothes on our backs, and for this we know we are truly prosperous. We give thanks for our riches.

"We also know, Great One, that you like it when we are active in our accumulation of the goods we desire. We know that you are happy we have the faith and confidence to be abundant, based on what good we can do and what service we can be to our friends, family, and our Mother Earth. We feel your strength when we believe we are worthy of such great gifts. We allow them into our lives, and we give thanks. We gather today to give praise and thanksgiving for the gifts we have received, and we are in agreement to allow even more goodness into our here-and-now experience. We agree to let our past be our past and move freely into this time of wondrous abundance and prosperity, and we give thanks for knowing we are also free and grand creators.

"Our hope, O Great One, lies in our faith and confidence in you, the Creator of all living things. We here today agree to give up worry, because it only binds our hands from doing the works you see fit for us to do. The People have many goals to accomplish, and we know the work ahead of us. It does not worry us, for whatever we desire, we know is done right here, right now, in your name, and we give thanks and praises. We now surrender the past to you and know it is the past. We are in great expectation of all the great gifts to come for all The People.

"We feel your presence and know that we are one with the Great Spirit, and we give thanksgiving. We agree to have the courage to move through our days with wonder and excitement. We know that true joy is in the experience of being here to share with our loved ones, and we place no importance on what we own, for it is only transitory. Our permanence lies in our love. Ah U Hop Vista Doogie Vista Doogie Ah He. God Bless You, God Bless us all. Thank you for this day."

All The People shook their heads in agreement, and everyone yelled out a big THANKSGIVING.

I learned from Leonard to truly be thankful. We do not have to wait for riches or great fortune to be thankful. If we look around us, we have plenty to be thankful for right now. How can we continually ask for more blessings when we do not give thanks for what has already been given to us?

O Great One and Leonard, I can never thank you enough. Thank you.

Jay and White Buffalo Speaks, Eastern Montana

Teepees on the RES. 1934, Shot by Miller

Chapter 25
The Painted Teepee

Once a very long time ago, there were two young braves who were out hunting. The two young men had just finished their vision quests and had become married, each one to a beautiful maiden. The boys had found their callings in their vision quests, and they were to be great tribal hunters and provide well for their new families and the people. Being friends and having a common purpose tied them together at the hip, so to speak, and they were almost inseparable.

While hunting out on the Great Plains for deer, they came across a rabbit, and they were about to kill it for food. The rabbit pleaded with them not to kill him, but to spare his life, and the two boys laughed and asked, "Why should we do such a thing?"

The rabbit replied, "Because I have a great gift for you, and I cannot give it if I am dead."

The young men looked at him with skepticism and asked, "Yes, and what is this great gift for which we should go hungry?"

"I can make you rich and successful hunters," the rabbit said.

"Oh, and how is that?" the young men asked.

"Go home now," the rabbit said, "and gather the colors of the desert on your way. Gather flowers from the mountains and soil from the earth. Grind these with water and clay and paint your teepees. It will bring you great luck. Adorn your teepees with beautiful colors and paint on them the totems you found in your quest. Your shelters will provide you with added warmth and protection and will bring good luck. Share this with the rest of your tribe and have all others in the Nations paint their teepees as well. You will become famous and very rich hunters for protecting The People of the Nations."

They did this and prospered dearly for many years to follow.

Walking the path and healing occasionally require surrender, as I was to find out. After twenty-four years of marriage to my own beautiful young maiden, my wife, Pamela, fell ill to cancer, and it did not take long for it ravage her body and take her to another place. Leonard loved Pammy very much, and he cried at her leaving. He said she was too young to leave us.

One day he said, "You know, my boy, some are just ready to leave this place earlier than others. Now she is gone from this place, but she is never far from you."

Leonard advised me to begin a new quest. "Teepee life would be good for you right now," he said. "Go find yourself a teepee, and paint it.

"Take your teepee down to your spot on the river. Get the young boys to help you set it up and leave you with paint. Apply your totems to the outside. Make the inside warm and comfortable because you are going to be there a while."

"But Leonard," I asked, "how I can paint my own teepee? Won't that bring me bad luck?"

"No," he said, knowing that I was referring to a tradition that only Natives should paint their teepees. "I am not blood," I said.

"It does not make a difference now," Leonard said. "You are my son, and the Creator will recognize this and not punish you for painting your teepee."

Leonard asked that I resign myself to teepee life for a period of time and not to speak with anyone for any reason. He said he would leave food and water near my camp so that I would not go hungry or thirsty.

"Go now, boy. Set up your camp. Pray, fast, and meditate every day. Fish for your trout on the Two Medicine River you love so well. Climb to the top of

Heart Butte and work on painting your teepee a little each day."

Living by myself in a teepee on the Res became a little lonely at times, and boring too, until I was able to quiet my mind, simply by saying, "Be quiet." It was frustrating at first, until my mind quieted and the pictures stopped racing through it, but I discovered that we have the ability to quiet the mind and to live self-sufficiently in peace with ourselves.

It became a peaceful time to see nature, to rest, to walk and hike, and to find there is really nothing to worry about, ever, because the Creator takes care of everything, even our loses and loneliness.

The loss of my wife and dear friends who had passed over at very young ages was not easy to experience, but teepee living helped me to heal and find my roots within myself.

"We often resist our natural need to grieve," said Leonard, "and we may not even recognize the signs of grief. Grief is a natural, normal and very necessary process. We cannot rush it or ignore it and retain our mental health. Grief has to be experienced, worked through, and resolved. "Cry out loud," Leonard advised, "and cry deep".

The loss of anything significant in a person's life—one's marriage, one's work, one's health, or a tremendous life change can all bring about grief.

"If you are grieving, let the grief come. Only when it has come can it be gone," said Leonard. "Go paint your Teepee," said Leonard, "it will bring you good luck".

I knew that was what Leonard wanted for me. He wanted me to have time to heal, to surrender to the quiet, and to find peace, love, and appreciation for life in my heart, and then I would be ready to move on. Life can be strange, in that sometimes you have to get away from it in order to live it.

I painted my teepee in earth colors with the totem animals I had come to know, the great Bear, the Eagle and the Squirrel, and I lived in it by myself on two different occasions for three months each time. I came to love the simplicity, the quiet, and the surrender of teepee life. I emerged from my quest knowing who I am and what I am here for. I now know my path, just as you will one day, I am certain.

Just Above My Spot on the Two Medicine River, 1997

On the Drive Back to Leonard's, Coming from Great Falls & Entering the Res

Chapter 26
Leonard's Views on the Environment

Up in the foothills over on the east side of the divide above Heart Butte, one can experience the vastness of Montana's wilderness. One has to visit Montana to understand why it is called Big Sky Country. The atmosphere combines with the terrain in a certain almost magical way to make the sky look twice as big as it does in most other parts of the country.

Leonard and I were out for a walk in the foothills, just a couple of miles above his house up near a crystal-clear lake called Greens Lake, a wonderful place to spend an afternoon and listen to Indian stories of long ago— also a great place to catch huge west slope cutthroat trout. Leonard was not a man that was easily fenced-in, and like most Natives, wanted the country around him big and open.

"Our people have hunted in these mountains for over 14,000 years that we know of. We used to be free to walk all the way into what is now called Canada and California," said Leonard.

"Under this grass, they tell us, lay huge amounts of resources that many large corporations would like to get their hands on, like the oil, gold, and silver. Big real estate developers would like to drop houses from the sky and move in people who do not know of the sacredness of this ground nor appreciate our Mother, who really owns this place.

"The People have known for many years about the oil under the grass and the gold too, and we know there are plenty of logging companies waiting for a decision from the U.S. government to issue permits that would let them come and cut the trees above our land boundaries, and to all of that, we have said, 'No, we do not want your gold, and we have no need for the oil you want to take from the ground, and we like the trees just where they are, and we do not want the Earth polluted from your mining.'"

In a dream, Leonard said he saw the rape and deterioration of the land. It was a nightmare that shocked him; he saw his own land developed into a "planned community" filled with new, expensive homes and many air-polluting automobiles driving all over the countryside. Shopping malls replaced open fields. Gas stations replaced ancient trees. The land suffered the same fate as so many *open spaces* before it, and became disrespected and trashed by its inhabitants—this made Leonard very depressed for a very long time following this dream.

"Mother asks that we hear her plea," said Leonard. "Mother asks that we hear her plea for a clean environment and a safe place for her children to play. Mother asks that we respect her and that we pay attention to her and care for her as she cares for us. Mother asked where else shall you dance?

"You have heard her words, Jay, through White Buffalo Speaks, and you know these words to be true. In this age, there are cars that run without the use of oil, and Mother Earth has told me, through our conversations, that she does not understand what people are doing underground, robbing her of her oil. She has told me this is dangerous," he said.

Leonard continued, "The water on the land of The People has become unfit to drink because of the runoff of so-called grey water from the big lodges above in the park lands. How easy it would be to clean that water by planting wild horseradish, if only of they would take the responsibility to do so. Your people," he said, referring to Whites, "have developed technology for this purpose, but large corporations have not seen enough profit to make the equipment to do the work.

"We do not want to mine the gold in these hills because we refuse to poison the water and the soil in the process of mining. Our Mother has suffered enough poisoning. The day for cleaning up this place has arrived," said Leonard. "We must move into a new time of conservation and find a way to burn less fuel and consume less energy, but your government does not want to talk of such things. These issues are under the control of the World Bank and large corporations managed by your government.

"How will The People ever be heard?" Leonard asked.

"I believe they will be heard one voice at a time," he said in answer to his own question. "There are many with the intention to educate, to stand up and say, 'We have had enough pollution and looting, and now is the time for reason.' Many good people have pleaded with big business and the government to stop poisoning our food with chemicals, and many have heard this plea.

"There are now more organic farms in America than anywhere else in the world, and this is a great lesson for the leaders in Europe, China, Africa, India, and Central and South America, as the people in these countries are also very large polluters. By this example, our Mother can be healed and, in the process, people all over the Earth can become more prosperous. Our true prosperity is the unfoldment of the soul," said Leonard, "not in the riches people rob.

"The importance of ridding our Mother of nuclear development has become well known, and the consequences of not doing so are no longer a secret. Your young geniuses have nearly invented mankind into non-existence with the vast use of microwave and cell phone communication. If they succeed, there will be no place to play the drum song or to dance or to sing to reach our souls unfoldment," said Leonard.

"The respect Mother wants and deserves is for all people in all lands to wake up and recognize her right to breathe, for her people to survive and prosper outside of slavery. Mother does not like being choked off by the smog in the cities," Leonard said. "She is tired of absorbing chemicals dumped on her land and in her waters. She asks the children of this land to find a way to love and respect and support her, and to stop trying to kill her.

"A change has got to come; there is no other way," he said. "Support those working to protect Mother Earth. Save a tree whenever possible. Don't throw your waste in the streets or dump it into her oceans. Nothing is more important, and then the unfoldment of the soul and this place offers us this great opportunity. There is no other place for this to happen," he said.

"Turn off an extra light. Stop watching TV. Find a way to love our mother and protect her before she is killed off forever. There is no other way," said Leonard.

"It all boils down to respect," said Leonard. "Mother Earth calls for our respect and love equal to her love for all the creatures that live here, and that includes mankind."

Today there are more people, foundations, and organizations working feverishly to help save our Mother from extinction. There are education centers being created all over the world, and The People have become proactive in loving, supporting, and respecting our Mother, and I know that Leonard is smiling.

Old Homesteaders Place Built in Early 1900's

Chapter 27
A Clear Mountain Morning
Of Nuclear Vision

There is something about the phone ringing at eight a.m. that makes me mindful of new beginnings. At eight a.m., my mind says, "It's time to embrace the day." I remember thinking that very thing one Friday morning in 1991 as the phone began to ring.

It was Leonard. He called to ask me to come over right away. Whatever it was, he said couldn't wait. I was always excited about getting to visit with him, but it was snowing like crazy. I said, "Leonard, it's been snowing like hell, man. Can we discuss this without me coming over? It looks pretty rough…"

The January snows in northwest Montana along the Great Divide can be treacherous, but Leonard's tone and his way of gently commanding came right through the phone that morning. "No, you need to come right away," he replied, and that ended our conversation.

"Pammy, I guess I'll take a ride over east this morning. Leonard has something important to discuss, and he says it can't wait. He asked me to come right away. Do you feel like making the drive with me?"

Pammy smiled and replied, "Jay, your time with Leonard is precious, and I'm sure he didn't say, 'Be sure and bring that pretty little wife of yours,' now did he?" She was enjoying this way of poking fun at me.

"Okay, but it would sure be nice to have you ride along over the pass," I said.

She replied in a more serious tone, "No, I don't want to interrupt whatever he has in mind for you. I'll pack you a lunch and some coffee while you get dressed. Now you go on."

And I did.

The drive over the divide that morning is hard to describe. There was an awesome beauty in the white treachery. January is the dead of winter in northwest Montana, and everything in sight is white, including where the road should be. In January, the elk are down low on their winter ground, but the mule deer can be a nuisance on the road. Whenever I stopped to inspect the road ahead or just to enjoy the scenery, it was easy to spot bald eagles flying overhead. That morning was no exception.

I watched closely, every movement around every bend, for mountain goat and big horn sheep at the road's edge licking the natural salts off any exposed rocks. In January, the animal kingdom hunts for live food and high grasses, all except the bear. They are smart enough to stay home and sleep.

The snowfall continued every mile. Visibility and road conditions deteriorated, as did my pace. It made the going slow, but the drive was beautiful, and nearly every mile I was reminded of the power that made us and keeps us alive through grace.

I could barely make out the shape of the corner of Leonard's house because of the crust of wind-swept snow. As I arrived, Leonard was bringing in wood for the night. He was a big, well built man and his strength and power seemed to be a part of his spirit.

"How was your drive?" he hollered from the corner of the porch.

"Long," I replied, and I kicked some of the snow from under the fender as I strode across the drive. "Snow was thick up on the pass, and I had to take it slow."

He was laughing out loud and pointing to his watch, "Slow? It's four o'clock! Thought for sure you'd decided to camp up on the pass. Oh by golly that would have been a rough night"

I quickly retorted, "Geez, Leonard, I'm pooped. What's on the stove?"

He kicked the door open with his boot and said over his shoulder, "Let's see what late arrivals get." He invited me to sit by the fire while he filled two bowls with thick moose stew. The house smelled with the rich aromas of wood fire and food.

"Bring any coffee?" he asked, knowing the answer.

"You bet. Do you think Pammy would ever forget your favorite? She wouldn't let me out of the house without it."

I continued, "Leonard, no disrespect, but what the heck was so important that I needed to come today?"

He answered, "Life, my boy, life. We'll talk tomorrow."

The morning light looked like the sun was on the third click of a three-way bulb. It was the brightest morning I'd ever seen. The sun blazed on the thick, new snow, which covered literally everything.

"Come out on the front field with me," Leonard urged. "Let's smoke a while."

If Leonard wanted to have a smoke, I knew he had something of deep significance to impart. It was his way of telling me to take seriously what he had to say.

"We have a choice," he began. "Right now, in our history on this planet, we have a choice to live or to die—and it's up to you and me to decide if our children and grandchildren will have a place to run and to play."

I heard a tone in his voice that brought goose bumps up on my neck and arms, and I asked, "Why now?"

What he told me nearly brought me to my knees.

"It came to me the night before last, just a few hours before I called you," Leonard replied. "The President is going to attack Iraq in the next few days. He is going to make war against dark-skinned people of far away, and one day this will lead to many more deaths, and then he will see that the war in the mind of many of your leaders is a war inside their heads. There is no war." He swept his arms up and out, spun around slowly in a circle and said, "One day, nuclear power will end all of this–even this very place."

We sat on a doeskin blanket that covered the snow on a large jutting rock as Leonard continued to describe his vision in which nuclear power was revealed to be the greatest evil on our planet. He said that even though nuclear power had the capability to end all of life on Earth, no one was talking about its danger.

He exclaimed, "The press won't talk about it because it is not news, schools won't talk against it because the teachers' hands are tied. The great leaders live like kings and gods while the rest of us toil in the sun, but they won't speak against it because their pockets are lined with gold from its potential killing."

I began to realize the depth and meaning of what Leonard was revealing to me, and I was certain that his vision had been very specific and clear.

"One day, madmen will blow up several of these nuclear power stations, and you will find that the End of Time, which your churches, New Age people, and the Hopi have spoken of, has come to pass. We people of the Blackfeet Nation do not believe in this end of time prophecy because we have always been fighters. We believe that every man can find goodness in his heart. We have always fought for what we believed was right for The People. Now we fight with thought, spoken words, pens and education."

He concluded his thought by bringing us back to the current day scenario. "Jay, we only have a short time to be effective in this war!" Leonard asked me again if I would choose life. I told him that I do choose life, and then he told me, "Then go out and let that choice be heard."

Leonard's forceful demeanor quickly changed into a serious urgency to tell others of the vision he received. He asked me, "How many people do you know?"

I replied, sensing he had more to impart to me, "I don't know. Do you mean The People of the reservation?"

"No," he replied, "people everywhere."

Leonard pleaded with me urgently, "You must write to the thousands that you know, call them, go visit them, bring them the message that the nuclear plants must come down. Let them know that time is very important. My vision gave us no more than twenty years to be here on this planet if the nuclear plants remain. Jay, you are my kindred. You must go with a

message of peace and love for all the people of the planet, for people everywhere. Ask men and woman to look into their hearts, and they will see the good and will act in a way that is their true way—only good. People know the difference between right and wrong, good and bad, and they must look into their hearts and live by what is there.

"Do blow dryers, microwave ovens, and two or three televisions in our homes justify the use of this deadly technology?" he asked. "How ignorant and shortsighted have people become?"

During our conversation, Leonard spoke of spiritual things, of temporal things, and of his own personal observations. He asked that we stop seeking God, stop trying to make ourselves happy, stop trying to figure out who we are. "We already know that," he said. "We are loving, spiritual beings here to experience life and to help others to do the same. That is our job. Now is the time to ensure the experience can go on. There is no other place for this to happen."

A Summer Storm Blew In at 4PM and Turned Day Into Night. It Blew Out Windows, and Several Hundred Trees Went Down; 1993

He said the vision revealed to him that we must help ourselves by thinking of future generations. He said that we must begin to do the things necessary to ensure that generations to come can experience life. He said that the vision had made it clear that this is to be the life work of each generation. "There is no other way," said Leonard.

Those morning hours with Leonard seemed like minutes, and his message was truly for the ages. His inner power was replaced by a larger urgency, a command, and a plea. "Nuclear power has the ability to destroy life for many thousands of years, and now it is your job and mine and every other responsible person's on this planet to disassemble it. There is nothing more important."

There were moments in Leonard's narration when he wept. "The Great Spirit has spoken with me and conveyed that there is no way around this. No way around it for the President, and for Presidents to come."

He continued, "The People of the Piegan Nation have always been warriors. We have fought bloody battles with opposing tribes and were the last to fight for Native American freedom in 1894. I could tell you many bitter tales of wars, killing and death, but that is not important now. Bloody war is not necessary to keep peace, love, and joy, and to survive. Peace and love between people must be so highly regarded that we would do anything to keep it, except war, and we must pass it on to all people—everywhere—no more war.

"We must go out into the world and spread this message of peace, as did your Jesus Christ over two thousand years ago. Now is a time of paramount importance for all people to hear the message of loving each other and our world, the message of being at peace with one another and our world, and the message of finding joy in each other and in our world."

I remember that beautiful, surreal morning with Leonard like it was yesterday. I remember walking back with him up to his front porch. He was exhausted from recounting the vision, from the emotion and the grim reality of it.

He asked me to hurry my communications to you. He asked us to turn out lights when we don't use them and to adjust our air-conditioning a few degrees.

He asked all of us to reduce energy consumption every single way we can and to go outside to enjoy our world, to take a walk, and to teach our children about our beautiful planet. Leonard asked us to look into the eyes of our children and think about what we are risking.

Before Leonard's passing in 1999, he had many visions, all of which were vivid and all of which came to pass. In the vision given to him about nuclear power, I have no doubt that Leonard saw the power plants being dismantled all over the world as well as vivid scenes of the consequences of their continued existence.

We have less than ten years left, according to Leonard's vision. I join Leonard in urging you to peacefully dismantle nuclear power plants and stations. Write to your congressman, write to your newspaper, go into the schools and talk about it, talk about it in the office, and scream about it in the streets. Spread the message of love, peace and joy—and no more war!

Dismantle the nuclear power plants now! It's up to you and me.

*Dear Great Spirit, Stricken Me All My Days To Be
Spent On This River"*

Chapter 28
The Future of the Tribe

"Human beings have been walking the Red Path for thousands of years, and they are just now coming into the realization of self and the unfoldment of the soul," said Leonard.

"One day all people will come to realize exactly who they are. They will come to know their own strength and power and will use it to be of great value and loving service. There is no other way," said Leonard. "The future of the tribe is obvious. It is to recognize our oneness with all tribes and come to know we are one spirit. The People of this nation, as with the people of the all other nations, have lived separately for many years and now, here in this place, we have come to find we cannot do so any longer. We are one," he said.

Leonard went on to say that once people reach deep inside and see the spark which reveals the mystery to unfoldment of the soul, they will automatically see this oneness. It is seated deep in the heart of their consciousness, and the light shall be seen by all one day. "Just close your eyes and look," he said.

"Humans have walked long in the shadow of darkness, where evil has lurked for many generations—many have made a deal with the devil, and now we are coming out into the light of day to see our own goodness, value, and worth—and to break the bond with evil and social injustice. The days of jealousy, hatred and greed are nearing the end of their time as people approach the light in their own hearts and lives. Soon there will be a day without wars, without famine, dis-ease, crime, stupidity and hatred. "Humans have come to recognize their own power in the spoken word and in thought and deed. In their unfoldment, they have found that a clean heart makes for clean hands. We have come to a place where when we look from our heart's center and exchange our ignorance for knowing and heartfelt communication. We have found in our knowing great strength and the courage to be of service and to lead the way to peace. There is no other way," he said.

"The day has come," he said. "It is here now, not in some dream of the future, but here now, when all people of all faiths and creeds and religions will walk as one, hand-in-hand in love, sympathy and mercy.

"The days of torture, malice, and insane killing have come to an end. All tribes have come to know how to love one another, live together and get along through the simple act of communication and understanding. We have finally learned how to drop our differences and live in perfect harmony and dance the Friendship Dance as one tribe. This has not been done under the guise of one world democracy, for that is not the true way; it is the mask of greed. The way of The People is love, for there is no higher purpose, and we have come to know this. There is no other way. When The People of the world come together and hear the drum song play, they will hear their hearts beat as it sings in this joy. Let us look at the alternative," he said. "People walking in ignorance and darkness, with only the love of money, jealousy, and greed in their hearts. They stand in their righteousness at our doorstep, armed with weapons of mass destruction and chemical warfare, defending their ignorance and their reasons to kill. Mass starvation, illness and disease in every nation, brought on mistakenly by man's need to kill and destroy. Children holding guns in their hands, and willing to take a life for fifty cents, is this the way?

Above the Blackfeet Res, in Canada—Blood Res 1990

"The world has long known of these things. A change has to come. People have seen the opportunity to step out of darkness and into the light, the light of truth, fairness and justice. The light of love, joy, and peace," said Leonard.

"We have witnessed the alternative for a very long time now and have chosen to live a new way, where children no longer go hungry and die of AIDS, where nations have come together and recognize the lack of intelligence of war, and express their willingness to have different opinions and allow different ideas to exist. We have come to live as one people on this planet, in peace and love with one another, as never before—knowing that God is too big for just one religion. There is no other way. Tribes of the world have to come together to live in love, peace and joy," he said. "Members of all tribes have come to realize there is no other way, for without this planet, there is no place to play the drum song. The People have been walking the Red Path for thousands of years in order to come into the unfoldment of the soul, and that unfoldment resides in our own awareness of who we truly are, Grand Creators, one with the Great Spirit."

Leonard is gone from this place now, but to this day, we remain as one. We are of one tribe, one with the Great Spirit creating love, peace, and joy.

Chapter 29

In Tribal Words

From Blackfeet Archives—with respect added to my book.

Siksika ('black feet', from *siksinam* 'black', *ka* the root of *oqkatsh*, 'foot'. The origin of the name is disputed, but it is commonly believed to have reference to the discoloring of their moccasins by the ashes of the prairie fires; it may possibly have reference to black-painted moccasins such as were worn by the Pawnee, Sihasapa, and other tribes). An important Algonquian confederacy of the northern plains, consisting of three sub tribes, the Siksika proper or Blackfeet, the Kainah or Bloods, and the Piegan, the whole body being popularly known as Blackfeet. In close alliance with these are the Atsina and the Sarsi.

Within the recent historic period, until gathered upon reservations, the Blackfeet held most of the immense territory stretching almost from North Saskatchewan river, Canada, to the southern headstreams of the Missouri in Montana, and from about lon.1051 to the base of the Rocky mountains. A century earlier, or about 1790, they were found by Mackenzie occupying the upper and middle South Saskatchewan, with the Atsina on the lower course of the same stream, both tribes being apparently in slow migration toward the North West (Mackenzie, Vov., lxx-lxxi, 1801). This would make them the vanguard of the Algonquian movement from the Red river country. With the exception of a temporary occupancy by invading Cree, this extreme northern region has always, within the historic period, been hold by Athapascan tribes. The tribe is now settled oil three reservations in Alberta, Canada, and one in North West

Montana, about half being on each side of the international boundary.

So far as history and tradition go, the Blackfeet have been roving buffalo hunters, dwelling in tipis and shifting periodically from place to place, without permanent habitations, without the pottery art or canoes, and without agriculture excepting for the sowing and gathering of a species of native tobacco. They also gathered the camas root in the foothills. Their traditions go back to a time when they had no horses and hunted their game on foot; but as early as Mackenzie's time, before 1800, they all ready had many horses, taken from tribes farther to the south, and later they became noted for their great horse herds. It is entirely probable that their spread over the plains region was due largely to the acquisition of the horse, and, about the same time, of the gun. They were a restless, aggressive, and predatory people, and, excepting for the Atsina and Sarsi, who lived under their protection, were constantly at war with all their neighbors, the Cree, Assiniboine, Sioux, Crows, Flatheads, and Kutenai. While never regularly at war with the United States, their general attitude toward Americans in the early days was one of hostility, while maintaining a doubtful friendship with the Hudson's Bay Co.

Their culture was that of the Plains tribes generally, although there is evidence of an earlier culture, approximately that of the Eastern timber tribes. The 3 main divisions seem to have been independent of each other, each having its own Sun dance, council, and elective head chief, although the Blackfeet proper appear to have been the original nucleus. Each of the 3 was subdivided into a number of bands, of which Grinnell enumerates 45 in all. It has been said that these bands were gents, but if so, their gentile character is no longer apparent. There is also a military and fraternal organization, similar to that existing in other Plains tribes, known among the Blackfeet as the *Ikunuuhkahtsi*, or All Comrades,' and consisting formerly, according to Grinnell, of at least 12 orders or societies, most of which are now extinct. They have a great number of dances-religious, wars, and social-besides secret societies for various purposes, together with many "sacred bundles," around each of which centers a ritual.

Practically every adult has also his personal "medicine." Both sexes may be members of some societies. Their principal deities are the Sun, and a supernatural being known as Napi, 'Old Man,' who may be an incarnation of the same idea. The dead are usually deposited in trees or sometimes laid away in tipis erected for the purpose on prominent hills.

As usual, many of the early estimates of Blackfeet population are plainly unreliable. The best appears to be that of Mackenzie, who estimated them about 1790 at 2,250 to 2,500 warriors, or perhaps 9,000 souls. In 1780-81, in 1837-38, in 1845, in 1857-58, and in 1869 they suffered great losses by smallpox. In 1864 they were reduced by measles, and in 1883-84 some 600 of those in Montana died of sheer starvation in consequence of the sudden extinction of the buffalo coincident with a reduction of rations. The official Indian report for 1858 gave them 7,300 souls, but another estimate, quoted by Hayden as having been made "under the most favorable circumstances" about the same time, gives them 2,400 warriors and 6,720 souls. In 1909 they were officially reported to number in all 4,635, viz: Blackfoot agency, Alberta, 795; Blood agency, Alberta, 1,174; Piegan agency, Alberta, 471; Blackfoot agency (Piegan), Montana, 2,195.

We Come From Right Here

For many years scholars theorized that the Blackfeet migrated east-to-west from the forests of the Great Lakes sometime in the last few hundred years. This was based on analyzing variations in Algonquin dialects (the Blackfeet language is classified by linguists as Algonquin) and concluding that we must have taken the language from east-to-west. Explanations for the Blackfeet's supposed migration ranged from the introduction of the horse and gun to conflict with other tribes.

But scholars write books and give lectures and huff and puff about times in which they never lived, worlds into which they never stepped foot, and languages they can never hear spoken by the ancients they study. As an example of how little is really known about Indians in the pre-Columbian period, experts can't even agree if the population of the Americas was 8 million or 112 million. If they know so little that they can't get within an order of magnitude of each other, why bother guessing about anything else?

Why, if it is generally agreed that Indians came across from Asia 12,000 or more years ago (which naturally means migration would occur south-to-north, and west-to-east) would anyone claim the Blackfeet must have migrated east-to-west?

In any case, anthropological theories aren't interesting to the Blackfeet. We know who we are and where we come from. **We come from right here.** We know, and have always said, that we have forever lived next to the Rocky Mountains. And we are right: recent archeological evidence shows that for thousands of years we have lived where we now live. There is a nearby buffalo jump that has buffalo bones mixed in with our bones that are over 14,000 years old.

Not that we needed any proof: Our Creation Story, handed down through a hundred generations, takes place at Badger-Two Medicine, a sacred place next to what is today the Blackfeet Reservation and Glacier Park. If a scholar wants to tell us that somewhere in the dark and distant mists of prehistory we walked from Asia, or came by raft across one ocean or another, we will listen and smile, because we like our Creation Story better.

From the time the white man came, and in fact *because* the white man came, our population has varied wildly, from perhaps 20,000 in the early 1800s, to possibly fewer than 2,000 in the 1890s, to over 16,000 today. Our grim mortality rate has been due to countless collisions between our tribe and non-Indians (Indians waged war on each other from time to time, but not necessarily to kill, and never with the aim of extermination). This is another way to say that left to our own abilities and able to make our own decisions, even in the most unforgiving of environments we have always flourished.

In 1837 smallpox was unwittingly brought by white men. Just ten days after visiting Fort McKenzie, Montana, the Blackfeet awoke to terrible and incurable symptoms of an unknown horror that quickly raged through the entire tribe. We lost 6,000 --half our tribe.

In the 1880s we came close to losing everyone to the Starvation Winter: Our numbers were diminished to perhaps less than 3,000. This occurred due to the near complete annihilation of the buffalo which represented 90% of our diet. (In the 1870s there we 5,000,000 buffalo on the Plains, five years later they were all but gone.) No one told us the buffalo had been wiped out until it was too late, and no one in Washington, D.C. truly understood how reliant we were on the animal. By the time the federal government realized its tragic mistake, we were dying in droves. Help came too little, too late, and if it weren't for the good people of Montana rushing us food across nearly impassible terrain, there might today be no Blackfeet Tribe at all.

And of course war with invading white soldiers, against whose numbers and guns we didn't stand a chance, depleted us in numbers, stature, and spirit at every turn.

In our "Dog Days" (when we use dogs to pull our travois from encampment to encampment) and into the horse and gun era which began about 1750, we relentlessly roamed the Plains following the enormous herds of buffalo. The moment our scouts came back with news of a herd, we would instantly pack up the entire camp and be in pursuit in a matter of minutes. The tipi enabled our mobile lifestyle, and that venerable lodge has never been improved on. In all the world, what other large, lightweight, portable home has proven equal to the tipi's unique ability to withstands prairie winds so powerful that a strong man can barely stand up, buffer its inhabitants from killing cold, and house a large family in such great comfort, yet be easily taken down or set up in minutes?

Before guns we used arrows and lances and sometimes allied with the Gros Ventre and Sarcee to fight our traditional enemies the Crow, Shoshone, Cree, Sioux, Flathead, and Assiniboin. Once we were mounted and armed with guns, we quickly came to dominate the Northern Plains, pushing the Shoshone, Kootenai, and Flathead to the western side of the Rocky Mountains, and every other challenger to distant domains.

Controlling such a large region, rich in wildlife, made us a natural and necessary trading partner for the fur trappers that started to appear in the mid-18th century. For over 100 years thereafter, trading with European trappers and traders was an important part of our economy and social lives.

But we had long been aggressive warriors and raiders, and so we would sometimes attack trading posts and raid settlements. This terrified settlers, so it was just a matter of time before governments and armies got involved. They were after our land in any case, and they would get it by hook, crook, or force. Our fearsome reputation gave them just the excuse needed to take a hard line with us. So before we knew what had happened we had ceded the vast majority of our lands to the federal government through treaties and other agreements that we were not equipped to negotiate or even understand.

The first treaty, known as Lame Bull's Treaty, was signed in 1855. More would follow, each taking huge chunks of our traditional land. We resisted as best we could, but retaliation was always disproportionate and murderous. In 1870, for example, a small confrontation sparked by the relentless, illegal encroachment of settlers and speculators resulted in the indiscriminate massacre of 173 women, children, and elderly by the U.S. Cavalry at Heavy Runner's Piegan camp on the Marias River. This was a peaceful camp under the protection of a safe conduct pass. It wasn't the camp the soldiers were hunting for. A Calvary scout named Kipp frantically shouted to the soldiers that this was the wrong camp and they were about to make a terrible mistake. But bloodlust and hatred cannot be diverted by right or reason, and this was our Wounded Knee, our Sand Hill.

In the end, as a small grace, we ended up with the land that was most sacred to us: our present day reservation. But this was not due to any sort of good will or best intentions on the part of the United States. The simple fact is that the land we wanted most was the land they wanted least.

In 1896 we had the Northern Rockies taken from us for a paltry $1.5 million because speculators believed there were rich minerals to be had. When mineral riches didn't pan out, this most sacred part of our homeland became Glacier National Park in 1910. As recently as 1925, Glacier National Park was still pressuring us to give up more land surrounding the Park.

To this day we question the legitimacy of the 1896 transaction. But thereafter, the modern-day reservation boundaries were essentially set, and lands within the reservation were allotted to individual Tribal members between 1907 and 1911 under the General Allotment Act. On the surface, the idea was to distribute reservation land to individual Indians, but in practice the Act enabled non-Indians to buy (or fleece) allotments from Indians or to purchase "excess lands." On some reservations, for example the Puyallup Reservation near Seattle, nearly all the land quickly left Tribal hands as it was purchased for pennies from Tribal members desperate for cash or seized for non-payment of taxes, and then developed into a drab and sprawling low- and middle-income suburb for non-Indians. Today, no one passing through the Puyallup Reservation would have the slightest notion they are on an Indian reservation, except for the occasional smoke shop or firework stand.

By comparison, the Blackfeet fared much better: Today, over 60% of the reservation remains in Tribal or Tribal-member hands, and the portions we don't own are generally very large ranches with few structures and fewer inhabitants. Our non-Indian ranchers are good neighbors and good stewards of the land, so the character and appearance or our rangelands has remained essentially unaltered since early times. Over 8,500 of the Reservation's 10,000 residents are enrolled Blackfeet. The other 1,500 are mostly Blackfeet descendants or Indians from other tribes, as well as a few hundred non-Indians.

In 1924, American Indians became U.S. citizens. In 1934, we became an "IRA Tribe" under the 1934 Indian Reorganization Act. This stemmed the tide of reservation land being sold to non-Indians by conferring trust land status on much of our acreage, and also formed the legal based for sovereignty, bestowed a measure self-governance, and provided a Tribal Constitution-based structure for our government.

Prior to the early 20th century it was uncommon for Blackfeet to be sufficiently skilled at writing to make good chroniclers for the Tribe. So, much of the best writings about us came from non-Indians that we welcomed into our world. Below are excerpts from an essay written in the 1930s by a longtime, trusted friend, a man named Frank B. Linderman. It's from his book: "OUT OF THE NORTH: A BRIEF HISTORICAL SKETCH OF THE BLACKFEET INDIAN TRIBE" and is a very good, lively, and romantic read. (Many Blackfeet would not agree with some of the statements made herein, but anyone who would take such trouble to learn about us and write so affectionately and sympathetically deserves to be heard uncensored.)

BLACKFEET! No tribal name appears oftener in the history of the Northwestern plains; no other is so indelibly written into the meager records of the early fur-trade of the upper Missouri river, and none ever inspired more dread in white plainsmen. Hell-gate* was not so named because the water there was fiercely wild, or the mountain trail difficult, but because the way led from tranquility to trouble, to the lands of the hostile Blackfeet. *Near Missoula, Montana-gateway through the Rockies to the plains.

The three tribes of the Blackfeet nation, the Pecunnies (Piegans), Bloods, and Blackfeet, are one people. They speak a common language, and practice the same customs. Long ago…they reached the wide plains bordering the Rocky Mountains in what is now Montana. Here they found vast herds of fat buffalo, elk, and antelope, an exhaustless abundance they had never known; and here, after driving the Snakes, and probably the Flatheads, Kootenai, and Nez Perces, from the bountiful grass-lands to the narrow valleys west of the Rockies, the three tribes of Blackfeet settled down to become plainsmen. Nobody can tell their numbers when they came out of the north. Old Pecunnie warriors have told me that their tribe once counted 750 lodges, probably less than 4000 people; and we know that, of the three tribes of the Blackfeet nation, the Pecunnie was the most numerous.

All this happened before the Blackfeet had horses. Dogs had always transported their goods. Now, to steal horses, their raiding parties ranged over the endless grass-lands far toward the south, old warriors say even into the Spanish possessions. Often these raiders were absent for two years; and nearly always they were successful. Their pony-bands grew until men measured their wealth in horses. Meat, their principal food, was easily obtained; and yet these people did not permit life to drag, or become stale. War and horse-stealing were their never-ending games; and besides furnishing necessary excitement and adventure they kept every man in constant training, since a successful raid was certain to bring attempts at reprisal. To be mentioned by his tribesmen as a great warrior, or cunning horse-thief, was the highest ambition of a Plains Indian; and the Blackfeet were master-hands at both these hazardous hobbies.

When finally they obtained fire-arms they became the scourge of the Northwestern plains, claiming all the country lying north of the Yellowstone River to the Saskatchewan. In stature they average taller than the men of neighboring tribes, having thin, shapely noses, and intelligent faces. Like the other tribesmen of the great grasslands they were naturally a deeply religious people; and like all the plains Indians they were naturally jolly, loving jest and laughter when not in the presence of strangers.

Even though the Blackfeet may have brought their social customs from the northern forests, they did not differ greatly from those of the other plains people. Each of the four tribes was subdivided into clans, or gents of blood kin in the male line, there being in the Blackfeet nation perhaps fifty such clans known as Black-Elks, Lone- Fighters, Fat-Roasters, White-Breasts, etc. A man was not permitted by tribal law to marry a woman who belonged to his own clan; and the children of any union belonged always to their mother's clan. Young women were closely guarded. There was little courting. Marriages were arranged by parents, with the consent of near relations. And yet, when possible, the desires of young people were given consideration.

Smoking was a sacred ceremony. Old plains Indians sealed oaths and agreements with the pipe. In smoking, the host or master of ceremonies, filled and lighted the stone pipe, offering its stem first to the sun (the father) and then to the earth (the mother) before smoking, himself. Next he passed the pipe to the guest on his left, "as the sun travels." After smoking, usually taking three deep draughts, this guest handed the pipe to the man on his left; the pipes stem being kept pointed at the lodge-wall in its movements. And the pipe must not be handed across the doorway. When the man nearest the door on the host's left hand had smoked, the pipe must go back to the "head" of the lodge where the host passed it to the guest on his right, the pipe going, unsmoked to the guest nearest the door on that side. When this guest had smoked he passed the pipe to the guest on his left, so that the pipe again began to move "as the sun travels." If the pipe needed refilling it was handed back to the host who replenished it, the guests passing it along, unsmoked, to the man who had discovered its emptiness. Nobody might properly pass between smokers and the lodge-fire.

Hereditary leadership was unknown. Men became chiefs by their prowess in war; and because he must ever be generous, a chief was usually a poor man. With the Blackfeet, as with the other Indians of the Northwestern plains, a chieftainship had to be maintained by constant demonstration of personal ability. It might easily be lost in a single day, since these independent tribesmen were free to choose their leaders, and were quick to desert a weak or cowardly character. This independence was instilled in the children of the plains people. They were never whipped, or severely punished. The boys were constantly lectured by the old men of the tribes, exhorted to strive for renown as warriors, and to die honorably in battle before old age came to them. The names of tribal heroes were forever upon the tongues of these teachers; and everywhere cowardice was bitterly condemned.

The girls were taught by their mothers and grandmothers to look seriously upon life, to shun the frivolous, and to avoid giggling. With the Blackfeet, women "gave" the sun-dances, the most sacred of their religious ceremonies; and because the "givers" of these sun-dances must have lived exemplary lives to have dared offer dances to the sun, they were forever afterward highly honored by both the men and women of the tribe. "Look, my daughter," a woman would say, "there goes Two-Stars. She is The-Sits-Beside-Him-Woman of White-Wolf. Two summers ago she gave a sun-dance, and she yet lives. If you try to be like her you may someday give a sun-dance, yourself."

The lodges, or tepees, of the plains Indians were the most comfortable transportable shelters ever devised by man. They were made of grained, and partially dressed, buffalo cow skins, from fourteen to twenty-four skins being required for a lodge. Indian women could easily pitch or strike a lodge within a few minutes. In cold weather the lodges were made comfortable, besides being brightened interiorly, by handsomely decorated linings which reached well above the heads of seated occupants, thus protecting them from draughts. From fourteen to twenty-six slender poles were required for each lodge, their length depending upon the height of the lodge. New sets of poles were usually cut each year, since dragging them over the plains in following the buffalo herds wore them out in a season. Lodges were often decorated with picture-stories of medicine-dreams, scalps, and buffalo-tails. In the village each clan, and each individual lodge, had its rightful position, the lodges of clan chieftains being pitched in a small circle within the village-circle, each always occupying its hereditary post.

Indians of the plains respect dignity and love formality. Conventional decorum, easy and masterful, was always evident in the lodges of old plains warriors. From the host's place at the "head" of a lodge his sons sat at his left, according to age; his wives, and their visiting women friends, on his right. A male guest, upon entering a lodge, turned to his right, around the lodge-fire, and was promptly assigned a seat on the host's left, according to his rank as a warrior. If a visitor had a message he stood while delivering it; and he was never interrupted for any reason until he had finished speaking, and had so declared. Once within a lodge even an enemy might speak as he chose without interference or heckling. After leaving the village he must look out for himself, however.

Basketry and the making of pottery were unknown to the Blackfeet. Their weapons, clothing, and robes received most of their artistic attention, the three-pronged design representing the three tribes of the nation being commonly used. Most of their bows were made of ash, or the wood of the chokecherry, their arrows being made of the shoots of service-berry bushes. Their shields were of rawhide taken from the necks of old buffalo-bulls. They would turn an arrow, and are said to have often turned bullets fired from old-fashioned rifles. The old time pipes of the Blackfeet were made of black, or greenish, stone, "straight" pipes sometimes being used in ceremonials.

The men wore shirts, breech-clouts, leggings, and moccasins, the latter soled with rawhide. In summer they wore no head-gear unless attending a ceremonial. In winter the men often wore caps made from the skins of animals or water-fowl. Eagle feathers were often worn by the men, beautiful war-bonnets being made with them. The women wore gowns of dressed deer, antelope, or mountain-sheep, skins that reached nearly to their ankles; and they also wore leggings, moccasins, and decorated belts carrying knives in painted scabbards.

The men were thorough sportsmen, loving horse-racing, foot-racing, and gambling. They were graceful winners, and good losers in games of chance. And they were firm believers in luck, and in the medicine conferred in dreams. Men often starved, and even, tortured themselves, in preparation for desired medicine-dreams. Then, weakened both physically and mentally by enervating sweat-baths and fatigue, they slipped away alone to some dangerous spot, usually a high mountain-peak, a sheer cliff, or a well-worn buffalo-trail that might be traveled at any hour by a vast herd of buffalo; and here, without food, or water, they spent four days and nights (if necessary) trying to dream, appealing to invisible "helpers," crying aloud to the winds until utter exhaustion brought them sleep, or unconsciousness—and perhaps a medicine-dream.

If lucky, some animal or bird appeared to the dreamer, offering counsel and help, nearly always prescribing rules which if followed would lead the dreamer to success in war. Thereafter the bird or animal appearing in the medicine-dream was the dreamer's medicine. He believed that all the power, the cunning, and the instinctive wisdom, possessed by the appearing bird or animal would forever afterward be his own in time of need. And always thereafter the dreamer carried with him some part of such bird or animal. It was his lucky-piece, a talisman, and he would undertake nothing without it upon his person.

In each of the three tribes of Blackfeet there were several societies, some of them being secret organizations. Most of them were military in character, some of them originally having police power over villages; and at least one of them was composed of boys who were not yet old enough to go to war. The Horn society of the Bloods, and the Kit-Foxes of the Pecunnies, seem to have been much the same society; and it may have been the most honorable and exclusive. The women of the Pecunnie also had a society which is said to have been secret. It was evidently not unlike the Horns in standing, since none but women of middle-age whose lives were known to have been upright were eligible to membership. This society selected its members, electing them before solicitation, one dissenting vote excluding a proposed woman.

Like all Indians of the plains, the Blackfeet formerly placed deep faith in the medicine-men, the "wise-ones" of their tribes; and even though these men resorted to intricate ceremonies which fascinated patients and onlookers there is no doubt that they often healed the sick and wounded through this faith alone. They did, however, possess considerable knowledge of the medicinal properties of herbs and roots, and often prescribed them. There was little sickness, since the daily lives of the plains Indians kept them in perfect physical condition. Sunrise saw most of the men and boys in the icy streams, winter and summer alike.

Burial of the dead was usually on platforms lashed to the limbs of trees beyond the reach of wolves. Securely wrapped in buffalo robes, firmly bound with rawhide thongs, the bodies were safe from ravens, crows, and magpies. Weapons and pipes were buried with warriors, root-diggers and cooking utensils with the women. Often a number of horses were killed at the burial of a warrior, so that his spirit might ride in The Sand Hills, the Heaven of the Blackfeet. In mourning for a son, or other male relative, both men and women scarified themselves, and cut off their hair, the women wailing piteously, sometimes for long periods. The mourning for women was of shorter duration, and not so wild.

The Blackfeet were meat eaters. Meat constituted fully 90% of their daily fare. It was either boiled or roasted, "meat-holes," which operated as fireless-cookers, being sometimes used. Roots and bulbs were also cooked in the ground; and the eggs of water-fowl were often steamed. Berries were eaten fresh; and they were dried for winter use, the latter being used in making the best pemmican, a mixture of dried, lean meat thoroughly pulverized and seasoned with the berries and bone-marrow. Ordinary pemmican was made with dried meat and melted tallow, no berries being used. The Blackfeet did not have salt, and like all the plains tribes dried their meat in the sun, unsalted, packing it away for winter use, the pemmican in buffalo-skin bags.

In the days before the white man came to the plains the Blackfeet were a happy people. An abundance of material for their food, clothing, and sheltering lodges was constantly in sight on every hand. Beyond these necessities their needs were few, so that with a firm belief in the exhaustless bounty of their loved grass-lands these practical folks lived each day for itself. And they knew how to live. Their pride in themselves forbade too much ease, even in their land of plenty. No successful hunter, no tribesman who, with crude weapons, plentifully fed a family, could have been a lazy man, no perfect horseman a weakling. The arms and wrists of men who could send arrows down to their feathers into the bodies of huge buffalo bulls were as powerful as spring steel; and men who loved war for its excitement could not have been weak-hearted.

The power of endurance of the plains Indians has always been beyond comprehension by white men. These tribesmen hunted, feasted, gambled, and eagerly made war, young men often faring forth alone over the unmarked plains to count coup, so that they might marry the young women of their choice, and be numbered among the tribe's warriors. Killing and scalping an enemy did not entitle them to count coup. They must strike an armed enemy with their hands, or with something held in their hands, without otherwise injuring the enemy; or they must capture an enemy's weapons, or be first to strike an enemy who had fallen in battle, etc., the rules for coup-counting differing somewhat among the plains tribes. And this coup-counting was expected of young men. For centuries, during the long, winter nights on these northern plains, red patriarchs feelingly extolled bravery and fortitude, reciting hero-tales, some of which may have had origin in far lands.* They were a change- less people, a romantically happy people, until the white man came to the plains. * I once found one of them in a translation from the Sanskrit.

The Blackfeet instinctively opposed the coming of white trappers and traders. Nevertheless the fur companies built forts on the upper Missouri in the heart of the Pecunnie country; and nowhere has the white man stooped so low for gain as in the fur trade of the Northwest; nowhere has he been so reprehensible as in his treatment of the Plains Indian. Besides his trade-whisky he brought infectious maladies to a people whose blood was clean. Nobody will ever know half the crimes that were committed by these avaricious traders. The enforced inoculation of a large band of visiting Indians with the virus of smallpox taken from the pustules on the body of a stricken white engages at Fort Union, whose blood was known to be otherwise unclean, is revolting enough, especially when one knows that the step was taken wholly in the interest of the traders who hoped to have the scourge over with before the fall trading began.

It is even more revolting when one learns that all the vaccinated Indians perished; and yet this deed is no more fiendish in character than the discharge of a cannon loaded with ounce trade-balls into a crowd of unsuspecting Pecunnies who were visiting at Fort McKenzie, a little below Fort Benton, in the year 1843.

The American Fur Company's steamboat. Trapper, brought smallpox up the river in 1837. This devastating scourge swept through the tribes of the Northwestern plains like a poisoned gale. Nobody knows how many Indians perished, estimates ranging from 60,000 to 200,000 men, women, and children. Perhaps the least of these figures is high. Nevertheless the Mandan's alone lost 6000 members, so that when the plague had spent itself the tribe had but 32 warriors left alive. Reaching Fort McKenzie the disease first attacked the inmates, deaths occurring so rapidly that burial was impossible. The dead bodies were thrown into the Missouri river. Within the fort there were 29 deaths, 26 of them being

Pecunnie women who had been attached to the forts engage. Upon the arrival of the disease-laden boat there had been 500 lodges of Blackfeet camped at Fort McKenzie. Now they were gone. During all the time that the smallpox had scourged the fort's company not an Indian appeared on the plains.

In October Alexander Culbertson, the American Fur Company's manager at McKenzie, set out to learn what might have happened to his patrons. He did not have to travel far before reaching a village of 60 Pecunnie lodges standing among the dead bodies of hundreds of men, women and children, and even of horses and dogs. Here, in these horrid surroundings, Culbertson found two old women, too feeble to travel, chanting their death-songs among the putrid dead. And here, having seen enough, Alexander Culbertson, the trader, turned back to his fort.

In November straggling groups of Blackfeet came to Fort McKenzie to tell their awful story. The disease had not made its appearance among them until the tenth day after leaving the post. Then its ravaging became so terrible that in the ensuing panic young warriors who fell ill stabbed themselves to death rather than have their fine bodies wasted and scarred by the loathsome disease. More than 6000 Blackfeet had perished, they said, more than half their nation. Many other tribes suffered as severely, the Assiniboins losing more than three-quarters of their warriors.

Nevertheless the trade in buffalo robes was that fall and winter greater than ever before at Forts McKenzie and Union, since dead Indians needed no robes. Stripped by thousands from their bodies by surviving tribesmen these death-robes were traded in at the Company's forts; and then, without the least attempt at disinfection, they were shipped to "the states" where, providentially, no epidemic of smallpox ensued. But the weakened tribes never again regained their numbers.

During all this time the heavy toll upon the immense herds of buffalo in the Northwest was scarcely noticeable; and now there was an exodus of traders. Having stripped the section of its beaver and land-fur, these avaricious white men began to abandon their trading-posts on the river, and to leave the country to the Indians and hungry wolves.

The Blackfeet, weakened in numbers, and tortured with bitter recollections, had scarcely settled down to their old life when the Seventies brought the professional skin-hunters to the plains. And now, for from 50 cents to $1.50 per head, these white men shot down the buffalo for their robes alone, leaving countless thousands of tons of fat meat to rot where it fell. By the middle Eighties the skin-hunters had finished. The buffalo were gone forever. The wide grass-lands, which for centuries had been so bountiful, were bleak, inhospitable, and bare. Even the elk and antelope had been wiped away. The Blackfeet, and all the Indians of the plains, were hungry now; and even while the Pecunnies searched in vain for the vanished herds, which the old warriors believed had hidden away, more than one-quarter of the tribe starved to death.

Dazed, unable to comprehend the terrible calamity which had overtaken them, clinging doggedly to their belief that the buffalo had hidden, and would soon return to their loved grass-lands, the Pecunnies were slow to rally. If the tardy Government of the United States had not acted the Pecunnies would have perished to a man.

But the Government did act at last; and the work of making wild hunters into gentle farmers in a single generation began. And this work is succeeding. The Pecunnies, and all the

Blackfeet, are rapidly becoming self-supporting by raising cattle and crops on the old buffalo range.

The Culture

American Indian culture has not only survived 150 years of intensive effort to eradicate it, it is once again flourishing and undergoing a rebirth, revitalization. This section looks at Blackfeet culture, past and present. But to understand our culture, or any American Indian culture, it is useful to understand *why* it has refused to die.

Through it all, we Blackfeet have remained a deeply spiritual people that have struggled to preserve and protect our culture, language, way of life, and way of thinking. We have an incredibly rich heritage of traditions, customs, beliefs, art, and stories. We have kept the flame of our culture alive through times when it was in constant danger of being extinguished. Today, thanks to our elders and ancestors who kept it flickering, the flame is burning brighter and brighter every year. It will soon be a blaze that will eventually outshine and outlive societies with shallower roots, a weaker notion of who they are and why they are here, and a lesser sense of obligation to the natural world, their community, and to each other.

Preserving our way of life has not been easy. Since the Europeans came, Blackfeet, like all Indians, have had to fend off non-stop attacks on our way of life, culminating in the late 1800s with the official government policy of assimilation. The assumption behind this misguided, paternal policy was that the white way of life was best, and therefore Indians should stop being Indians and start living, acting, and thinking like whites. In other words: "Become civilized like us, and you will be happier and better off."

So it was ignorance and a false sense of superiority, more so than malice that caused high-minded, urban easterners to make policies that created Indian boarding schools, forbade young Indians to speak their first language, and forced them to cut their hair and dress like whites.

It was ignorance because these policies overlooked two immutable facts: First, there never was anything intrinsically superior about the "civilized" lifestyle and worldview to begin with. Indians lived prosperously and successfully for thousands of years without ever making for themselves the problems Europeans made in far less time: genocide, disease, nonstop wars of conquest and religion, wholesale pollution of the earth, rigid class systems that disregard intellect and merit and trap vast segments of humanity in poverty and virtual slavery, political systems that oppress and leech upon all but the privileged few, science and learning whose main aim is to advance military technology or further an ideology, and a general view that man, not the natural world, is why the universe exists.

Second, for the reasons noted in the previous paragraph and for a thousand other reasons, **Indians like being Indians. Indians want to be Indians. Indians will always fight to remain Indians.** Our ancestors and elders did not want to be socially reengineered by people who never understood us to begin with, especially when our lives and societies were already better than the lives and societies of those who would reengineer us.

Completely lost on these would-be social engineers of the late 19th and early 20th centuries is this: If the purpose of America is "Life, Liberty, and the Pursuit of Happiness" who is fuller of life, freer, and happier than Indians left to live life as they see fit?

So the reason Indian tribes have survived and are today making a strong comeback —a hundred years after everyone thought they would have and should have disappeared— is simply this: Indians want to be Indians, they *must* be Indians, because our way of life is too good, too valuable, too important to let die.

The Blackfeet have a complex system of beliefs, some of which today may be as much unconscious as conscious. For example, in the past we avoided eating fish or using canoes because we believe that rivers and lakes hold special power through habitation of Underwater People called the *Suyitapis*. The Suyitapis are the power source for medicine bundles, painted lodge covers, and other sacred items.

So even today, a traditional disdain for fishing persists for many. We have some of the largest trout in the world in Duck Lake and other lakes and rivers, but it is visitors more so than Tribal members that do the fishing. And we have the most amazing and inviting lakes anywhere, right next to Glacier Park, but you won't find many of us on the water in boats.

Though we now generally live in houses to shield us from our brutal winters, most families have large Tepees that are built to a standard size and traditional design. Visit our huge, annual summer powwow called North American Indian Days and you will see an endless sea of Tepees, all about the same height and diameter. Painted tipis are sacred, each has a story and unique identity, may not copied or replicated, and can only be transferred by way of an elaborate ritual.

In the past Tepees were made from 8 to 20 buffalo hides. Today we use a heavy cloth because buffalos, like us, are making a comeback and a large number of hides are still hard to come by. In the past, about 19 pine poles, each averaging

18 feet in length, comprised a tipi's frame. That is pretty much the same today. We still prefer the strong and distinctive tall-but-thin lodge pole pines that are a found in the high elevations and short growing seasons of the Rockies.

True to our tradition of hunting buffalo, and later hunting elk and raising beef, red meat is a staple for us. We also still love dried meat prepared in the old ways. In the past, fish, reptiles, and grizzly bears were, except for a few bands, considered unfit for consumption. We still don't eat much fish or bear.

Our traditional music as played today is similar to many other tribes: drumming and singing. Traditionally, we used two types of drums. For the Sun Dance we used a section of tree trunk with skin stretched over both ends, much like the drums you see at powwows today. We also used something resembling a tambourine with hide stretched over a broad wooden hoop. Various types of rattles made of hides or buffalo hides were also used for various ceremonies. Whistles were also used in the Sun Dance.

In the past we made our clothing from the hides of buffalo, deer, elk, and antelope. Women tailored dresses for themselves from durable and pliable skins of antelope or mountain sheep. These dresses were usually ankle length and sleeveless, held up by straps, and decorated with cut fringes, porcupine quills, and geometric designs. After the traders came in the 18th century, glass beads were used to decorate clothing and other items. Women also wore necklaces of sweet-grass and bracelets of elk or deer teeth. Moccasins and (in winter) long buffalo robes, often decorated with earthen or plant dyes and elaborate porcupine quill embroidery, were worn by men and women.

Men wore antelope or mountain sheep leggings, shirts and breechcloths. They wore necklaces made from the claws and teeth of bears and from braided sweet grass. This dress was common among Blackfoot men until the last decade of the nineteenth century.

Today when you visit North American Indian Days or any traditional gathering on the Blackfeet Reservation, you will find us in our finest, most splendid clothing and costumes. You will see fine and fancy traditional Blackfeet dress as well as multi-tribal designs made purposefully to compete in the powwow circuit. And you'll see an array of more modern clothing infused with traditional elements and ornamentation.

In the past, we had numerous dance societies, each having a social and religious function. Dances reflected our emphasis on hunting and war and were usually held in summer. Members were honored in the dances for bravery, skill, or generosity. The Sun Dance was an annual sacred celebration of the sun, occurring in mid-summer. It was initiated by the "vow woman," a virtuous woman who vowed to take on the responsibilities of sponsoring the Sun Dance. The Sun Dance required the construction of a special circular lodge, and involved men fasting and praying, and dancing from the wall to a central pole and back inside the lodge. The Sun Dance lasted four days, and voluntary piercing of the chest for ritual purposes was sometimes a concluding feature of the dance.

Medicine bundles continue to be a central part of our ceremonial and spiritual life. These bundles were originally wrapped in rawhide, but today may be wrapped in cloth or hide. They usually contain the things needed to perform a particular ceremony or ritual, for example tobacco, pipe, paint, sweetgrass, beaver hide, war shirt, knife, lance, or other items. When treated in certain ways, these bundles have the power needed to perform our most important and spiritual ceremonies. Medicine bundles and the power they contain are commonly passed from one person to another in an elaborate ceremony when the time is right to do so.

We continue to practice many of the ancient ways, including the sweat lodge and vision quest, which involves fasting to make oneself weak in a remote place such as Chief Mountain, where we await a vision.

Our language is making resurgence, with numerous educational institutions on the reservation providing instruction. Ours is primarily an oral tradition but we have always kept a record of Tribal history and events by painting Tepees, robes, and hides with pictures to tell the story, something we do to this day. Hides painted to record the year's significant occurrences are called a winter count, and you will find winters counts mentioned in the "Historical Timeline" section of this website. Perhaps it is our tradition of visual imagery that explains why the Blackfeet have such an unusually large number of talented, internationally-celebrated artists.

Today many Blackfeet are Christians, but that doesn't conflict with our ancient sense of spirituality and the supernatural. "The entire Blackfeet universe," Malcolm McFee stated in *Modern Blackfeet* "was invested with a pervasive supernatural power that could be met within the natural environment."

We have always sought these powers, believing the life of the land and our own lives were irrevocably bound and intertwined. We hope that an animal's power or the power of a natural element will be bestowed upon us in a dream. The animal, often appearing in human form, might provide us with a list of the objects, songs, and rituals necessary to use this power. Then we should gather the objects into a medicine bundle and do what we have been told to do to avail ourselves and others of the power.

All this may sound strange to you, but to a Blackfeet standing on the reservation it would sound stranger to suggest there is *not* a supernatural power running through us and everything around us. We feel it, and perhaps you will too when you come to visit.

"The world of the Blackfeet, their entire universe, is inhabited by good and evil spirits. The realm of the supernatural is accepted as a significant part of everyday life, without the need to analyze or rationalize it. They believe in the "Sun Power" as the source of all power. It is everywhere; in the mountains, lakes, rivers, birds, and wild animals, and this power can be transferred to people. The gift, usually in the form of songs, comes through the medium of some animal, bird, or supernatural being, whose pity for the person comes when the person demonstrates his need through fasting. The songs received are means to contact the spirit powers. The power bestowed can heal the sick and make all things new again.

Thank you Pammy

Thank you Leonard

Harvesting Sage in praises of Leonard and Pammy

Brothers & Sisters we gather here on this Sacred ground

In Praises and Thanksgiving
We come together to smoke the pipe in praises and
thanksgiving, we gather to pray and to be heard. We have
gathered here for thousands of years and our tradition is
unchanged and unbreakable. We come in peace and ask that
our words be heard.

Grandmother, Grandfather from which we came thank you,
thank for allowing us to be people, thank you for our gifts
today. We say hello in deep love to the tree and rock People,
thank you for the fresh water in the streams great ones.
Thank you for the fresh air we breathe today. As we gaze up
to Geronimo rock and Squaw rock we see ourselves in them-
steady, strong and patient.

My brothers and sisters here today come with prayers for
healing, prayers for their family and other loved ones.
Grandmother, Grandfather may their prayers be heard and
answered, and my they walk here barefooted in praises of
this land and feel your power and grace.

Grandmother, Grandfather we have been walking, sitting, laying and praying in this very spot for thousands of years- we call it home, even though we live wherever we are at the time. Home tree is our spot and we hold you in high regard here. Grandmother, Grandfather takes pity on us. We ask the great ones who have walked here before us that we in unison feel and practice Love, Peace and Joy and in you we are that. We ask the Feather People, Bear People and Wapiti People be proud to have us visit this day and ask that they be blessed today with their presence. Grandmother, Grandfather we are human beings we do the very best we can. At times we may not understand and we know there are great mysteries we will never know. In our humanness we err.

Take pity on us and show us our way. That no matter what we might experience that we accept it easily and in Love, Peace and Joy-for this experience we are truly grateful and give praises and thanksgiving.

Today a wild flower unfolded herself as a beauty queen and in that we know everything is perfect all of the time. Thank you Grandmother, Grandfather for this wondrous place we are allowed to call home-even for just a short while. Great ones, wisdom walkers, saints, angels and most high achieved ones-thank you. Thank you for our lives, our abodes, and the foods we put in our bellies and share with our loved ones. Thank you for everything without you this nor we would be here. Thank you for the breath of life, thank you for the spark of creation that keeps us alive and in this place.

We will come together many more times to give thanks and praises to the great ones that have lead us here today. In ever deeper love and appreciation we will turn to the east and give thanks, we will turn to the west and give thanks, we will turn to the north and the south and each time we give thanks as it

goes even deeper into our hearts. Thank you for this Earth, thank you for this fire, thank you for this wind and water. In this place we have come to know your power and strength- and we know we are one with you, thank to Grandmother, Grandfather for the creation of abounding beauty.
Thank you for our healing today, Aho

Au Ho Hop Vista Doogi, Vista Doggi Ahe he
Blessings, Blessing from the Creator
In Deep love and gratitude
Jay North aka J. Mountain Chief

One day you will come to this sacred ground…

Other Books by Jay North

Available through www.OneGlobePress.com

Thoughts Without Thinking

Open Spaces-The Final Chapter

Health and Beauty Secrets of the Stars N/A

Advanced Breakthroughs in Massage Technology N/A

The Windowsill Organic Gardener: Organic Growing for the Urban Gardener

Getting Started in Organic Gardening for Fun and Profit

Open Spaces: My Life with Leonard J. Mountain Chief, Blackfeet Elder from Northwest Montana

Grow Yourself Rich, a book about marketing organic produce or any product, for that matter

Guide to Cooking with Edible Flowers, a self-published guide that sold 100,000 copies **N/A**

The Gift of Touch, a book on massage and energy healing

How to Cure and Prevent Baldness, a Beauty and Barber Industry Booklet

Miracles in the Kitchen—comprehensive data on healing and healthy living

Life and Times of a Hollywood Hair Dresser, Confessions of a Hollywood Hair Dresser—a work in progress

Coming Soon, four New Books: by Jay North

Walter's Big Adventure II, by Walter

Open Spaces—The Final Chapter—It is Done! Finally.

Living Off the Land Organically

What Really Happened? The True Story of the Sixties

Open Spaces:
My Life with Leonard J. Mountain Chief,
Blackfeet Elder from Northwest Montana
Spirit Talk by Jay North aka J Mountain Chief

WALK YOUR PATH WITH REVERENCE

Made in the USA
San Bernardino, CA
09 March 2020